**COLLINS GEM**
# CATS
*a mine of information*

C000174842

**COLLINS GEM**
# HORSES
**& PONIES**
*a mine of information*

**COLLINS GEM**
*a mine of information*

**KINGS &
QUEENS**
*a mine of information*

**& TOADSTOOLS**
*a mine of information*

**COLLINS GEM**
# SNAKES
*a mine of information*

**COLLINS GEM**
# SPIDERS
*a mine of information*

**COLLINS GEM**
# STRESS
**Survival Guide**
*a mine of information*

**COLLINS GEM**
# TAROT
*a mine of information*

**COLLINS GEM**
# WINE
**Guide**
*a mine of information*

**COLLINS GEM**
# WORLD
**atlas**
*a mine of information*

**COLLINS GEM**
# YOGA
*a mine of information*

**COLLINS GEM**
# ZODIAC
**Types**
*a mine of information*

# REFLEXOLOGY

**Nicola Hall**

HarperCollins*Publishers*

The right of Nicola Hall to be identified as the
author of this work has been asserted by her in
accordance with the Copyright, Designs and
Patents Act 1988

HarperCollins*Publishers*
103 Westerhill Road
Bishopbriggs
Glasgow G64 2QT

First published 2001

Reprint 10 9 8 7 6 5 4 3 2 1 0

© Essential Books 2001
All photographs © Nicola Hall

ISBN 0 00 710145 7

Printed in Italy by Amadeus S.p.A

# Contents

# Introduction

Reflexology is increasing in popularity as more people turn towards natural forms of medicine. Now more than ever before, individuals are taking responsibility for their own health, and as well as becoming more conscious of healthy eating, exercising and relaxing, more and more people are trying out complementary therapies. People are also more worried than ever about the possible side-effects of the powerful medicines that their doctors are prescribing.

Of those people who turn to complementary therapies, some visit the doctor for a diagnosis of their problem and then decide to try a natural therapy before or in conjunction with a course of conventional medical treatment. However, a growing number of people are trying complementary therapy before visiting the doctor if their complaint does not seem too serious. It must be stressed, though, that the responsible reflexology practitioner will not discourage patients from seeing their doctor, and there will always be times when it is essential to do so.

With the increased popularity of the method there are occasions on which reflexology is available from the NHS, but in general the treatment is provided by private practitioners.

# Self Treatment

## RECOGNISING IMBALANCES

When a part of the body is not working to full efficiency, a tender area will be found in the corresponding part of the foot when pressure is applied to it. By working this area over a period of time, the tenderness should reduce as the part of the body begins to function correctly again.

Reflexology involves treating the body by applying massage to reflex areas found in the feet and hands. It is more common for the feet to be worked on than the hands. Self treatment is possible, but caution should be exercised in this case. Beginners should not attempt self treatment if they have a serious condition which might be aggravated by it. That said, provided you are fairly flexible and can reach your feet, it should be possible to see the different areas of the feet and apply pressure to them with the thumbs and fingers. By referring to the reflexology chart, you can identify which areas of the foot relate to particular areas of the body.

The feet reflect the whole body, with different areas of the feet corresponding to all the parts of the body. The right foot corresponds to the right side of the body and the left foot to the left side.

Ideally with reflexology, a full treatment is always given to all of the areas in the feet, thus treating the whole body. This allows not just one symptom to be treated but the causes of that symptom too. It also means that a number of different symptoms can be addressed in a single treatment.

> Common mistakes with self-treatment are working too heavily on the different areas and working for too long on them.

# Holistic Approach

By covering all the reflex areas, the treatment will be 'holistic', which is the concept behind nearly all of the complementary therapies. To apply a holistic approach is to treat the body as a whole. This means treating not just on a physical level but also on an emotional and even a spiritual level. The effects of reflexology can be far-reaching.

Although it is possible to give treatment to isolated parts of the foot, the best results will be achieved when a full treatment is given to both feet. Although the method sounds simple, the results can be striking and, as the following should show, reflexology is much more than 'toe tickling'.

# The History and Theory of the Method

## ANCIENT CHINA

Reflexology is not a new therapy. It is generally agreed that its origins lie in ancient China. Methods such as acupuncture and various pressure therapies have been practised in China for thousands of years, and a Chinese medical book attributed to Hwang Ti, who died in 2598 BC, contained information on 'the examining foot method'. There is also evidence to suggest that in AD 1017 a Dr Wang Wei treated the sick by sticking needles into important acupuncture points on the body and then applying deep pressure therapy to the soles of their feet, before concentrating pressure on the big toe.

## ANCIENT EGYPT

Early evidence of a method similar to present-day reflexology is found in a tomb drawing at Saqqara in Egypt. The tomb, dated 2500 BC, is that of Ankhmahor, a highly respected physician. It includes six wall drawings, one of which shows four men. One man is applying pressure with his hand to the foot of another, and a third man is applying pressure with his hand to the hand of a fourth. Above the men, the hieroglyphics show the 'patient' saying 'Do not let it be painful' and the 'practitioner' replying 'I do as you please'. It is thought that the method spread from Egypt to Greece, Arabia and then to Europe.

## THE REFLEXOLOGY OF INDIA AND THE NORTH AMERICAN INDIANS

It is also known that a method similar to reflexology was used in India more than 5000 years ago. In addition, ancient footprint carvings and paintings have been identified that clearly show the soles of the feet with symbols on different parts of the foot relating to different parts of the body.

It is also known that North American Indian tribes have used foot therapy, although no written evidence exists. Cherokee Indians have told of their people using reflexology as a healing method, and of how this method has been passed down from generation to generation.

## MODERN REFLEXOLOGY AND ZONE THERAPY

Modern-day reflexology was developed from a method known as 'zone therapy'. This was first described in 1917 by an American ear, nose and throat consultant called Dr William Fitzgerald. It is thought that he came across the method while studying in Europe. Fitzgerald found that if he applied firm pressure to particular areas in the nose, mouth, throat and tongue, sensations could be deadened in specific areas. More relevant to reflexology was his finding that pressure exerted on parts of the hands, feet or over the joints produced similar results and relief from pain elsewhere in the body. The first use he made of this was as a means of anaesthesia during treatment or even surgery.

The work of Dr Fitzgerald was developed further by another American, Dr Joe Shelby Riley, and it was through Dr Riley that Eunice Ingham, widely considered to be the pioneer of modern-day reflexology, was first introduced to zone therapy in the early 1930s. Eunice Ingham was the first to identify the feet as the main area to which pressure should be applied for pain-killing effect and to treat illnesses. She developed what was called the 'the Ingham Method of Compression Massage' and was the first to call the method 'Reflexology'. She was also the first to write a book on foot reflexology, which was called *Stories the Feet Can Tell*. This was first published in 1938 and was followed in 1951 by *Stories the Feet Have Told*.

## DOREEN BAYLY AND THE BAYLY SCHOOL

The work of Eunice Ingham was first introduced to Great Britain in 1960 by Doreen Bayly. Mrs Bayly had met Eunice Ingham in America and studied with her before returning to Great Britain to practise and teach the method. Mrs Bayly did a tremendous amount of work in introducing reflexology in Great Britain at a time when complementary therapies were not so popular. She also taught many students in Europe and her teachings are continued by the Bayly School of Reflexology.

As treatment by reflexology has become more accepted, offshoots of the original approach have now developed. Variations in the pressure used, such as with 'light touch' reflexology and, at the other extreme, a very heavy pressure with 'advanced reflexology techniques', have been introduced together with 'precision reflexology' and 'vertical reflex therapy'. Reflexology involves treatment to the feet and sometimes the hands, but some practitioners now also practise a method called ear reflexology. The different approaches each have something to offer, but the basics should be learnt first.

# How Reflexology Works

Many theories have been put forward about how reflexology works as a form of treatment. As yet there is no sound scientific evidence relating to precisely what happens when pressure is applied to a particular part of the foot and causes a response in a distant part of the body.

## The Longitudinal Zones

Dr Fitzgerald divided the body into ten longitudinal zones with each zone extending from the toes up the legs and up through the body to the brain and then down the arms to the fingers. An imaginary line drawn through the centre of the body will give five zones on the right side and five zones on the left with each zone being of equal width at any level in the body, so that as the body gets wider so the zones also widen. These zones are thus segments through the body, not fine lines like acupuncture meridians. Zones are numbered according to which toe or finger they are in line with.

Zone therapy involved applying pressure to a part of the body to influence the functioning of other parts situated in the same longitudinal zone but distant from the part of the body

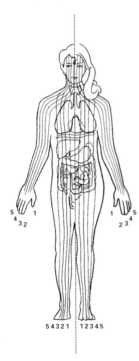

**Zone 1** is from the big toe up the inside of the leg through the body to the brain and down the inside of the arm to the thumb;

**Zone 2** is from the second toe, up the leg through the body to the brain and down the arm to the second finger;

**Zone 3** is from the third toe, up the leg through the body to the brain and down the arm to the third finger;

**Zone 4** is from the fourth toe, up the leg through the body to the brain and down the arm to the fourth finger;

**Zone 5** is from the little toe, up the outside of the leg and body to the outer side of the brain and down the outside of the arm to the little finger.

to which pressure was applied. By applying pressure to a zone, it was considered that any disturbance or energy block within that zone could be cleared and, with the correct flow of energy, the body parts in that zone would function correctly. Fitzgerald would use gadgets to apply the pressure, including rubber bands (wrapped around the fingers), clothes pegs (clipped to the fingers or toes), metal combs (pressed into the palms) and metal clips (placed on the fleshy parts of the body such as the abdomen). The gadgets would apply prolonged pressure and the patient would be told to release them only when the area to which they were applied turned blue.

A similar theory applied to reflexology, but with pressure applied using the thumbs and fingers and by working only the feet in order to correct the imbalances in the body.

# The Acupuncture Meridians

A theory held by some therapists is that reflexology does not in fact work on the longitudinal zones but along acupuncture meridian lines. This theory is probably best attributed to Danish practitioner Mrs Inge Dougans. Her book *The Art of Reflexology* introduced the theory and describes the relationship between the meridians and the reflex areas.

For the method of acupuncture, the body is said to contain twelve pairs of meridian lines which travel within the body, though not in straight lines like the ten areas of zone therapy described by Dr Fitzgerald. These meridians start or end in the hands or the feet. The Chinese believe that the vital life energy, ch'i, circulates through the body along these meridian lines in a similar manner to blood flowing within the circulatory system. The meridians are a combination of positive and negative energies, either yin (negative) or yang (positive) depending on which way the energy flows. If the energy is flowing freely through the meridians the body will function correctly, but when there is a blockage in the energy flow, illness results. By inserting needles at certain points along the meridian lines, the method of acupuncture helps to balance the flow of energy.

Those people who hold that reflexology works in a similar way to acupuncture believe that by applying pressure to points in the feet situated on the meridian lines energy will be balanced throughout the body. Certainly when working the zones of the feet, there will be an overlap with some of the meridian lines and therefore some influence on this energy system will be achieved. Whether the two methods work on the same energy system has not yet been established.

# The Central Nervous and Circulatory Systems

Other theories revolve around the effect of reflexology on the nervous and circulatory systems. Those who dismiss the idea that there are energy lines in the body think that reflexology operates through the nervous system, with nerve pathways existing between reflex areas in the feet and the distant parts of the body. They maintain that set reflex pathways must exist which bring about the results experienced in reflexology.

The circulatory system is also important. The blood which is circulated around the body in the blood vessels transports nutrients and oxygen to the different cells and tissues. The blood also transports waste products to the parts of the body which will get rid of them.

Possible effects on the circulatory system are as follows:

- A feeling of warmth after treatment due to increased blood flow.

- Looking flushed due to increased blood flow.

- A feeling of coldness during or by the end of treatment.

The latter indicates that blood flow is being directed inwards to help the healing process.

# The Body's Healing Forces

Another theory involves the idea of healing forces within the body. With many minor illnesses, a person will recover without treatment, since the body has a great capacity for putting itself back in order if things go wrong. Some believe that reflexology helps stimulate those healing forces and encourage the body to put itself back into working order.

One of the appealing aspects of reflexology is that it is the most natural of natural therapies, since the treatment does not involve taking any medication or using needles or other gadgets. It is carried out entirely using the touch of the practitioner on the feet of the patient.

Like all alternative therapies, reflexology attracts a certain amount of cynicism from those who dismiss its success as a placebo effect. There is evidence to suggest that for around one in three patients the feeling of being healed is indeed 'all in the mind', but this does not justify dismissing it, since the aim of any therapy is to make a person feel better.

It is hoped that in the future science will show what happens when pressure applied to a part of the foot has an effect on another part of the body. The effectiveness of treatment is known to the many who have benefited from it but scientific evidence would be helpful to convince the non-believers.

# THE REFLEX AREAS OF THE FEET

All of the parts of the body can be represented in the feet, and specific areas of the feet called 'reflex areas' are arranged in such a manner that a map of the body can be found in the feet. These 'reflex areas' are located on the soles, the two sides of the feet and the tops of the feet. The right foot corresponds to the right side of the body and the left foot to the left side, so parts of the body which are paired and found on both sides of the body will be represented in both feet – e.g. the right eye in the right foot and the left eye in the left foot. Parts of the body found on just one side of the body will be represented in the corresponding foot, e.g. the gall bladder (found on the right side of the body) will be represented only in the right foot, and the spleen (found on the left side of the body) will be represented in the left foot.

Reflexology can be especially helpful in reducing stress. The majority of people who consult practitioners for reflexology treatment come with stress-related conditions and for the vast majority of those the treatment is beneficial.

# Longitudinal Zones

Based on the ten longitudinal zones described by Dr William Fitzgerald, for each body part contained within a particular zone or zones, there will be a corresponding reflex area in the same zone or zones of the feet.

# Transverse Zones

Another system of zones that can be helpful in determining the position of reflex areas are the transverse zones first identified by German practitioner Mrs Hanne Marquardt. She described the existence in the body and in the foot of three transverse zones. These zones relate to :

**1.** the level of the shoulder girdle

**2.** the waist level

**3.** the level of the pelvic floor

She identified how these transverse zones could be related to the skeleton of the foot:

# Transverse Zones in the Feet

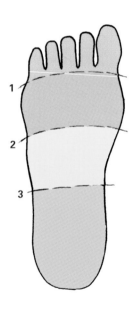

**1.** The first zone is at the base of the phalanges where they meet the metatarsals, and this relates to the level of the shoulder girdle.

**2.** The second zone is at the base of the metatarsals where they meet the tarsals, and this relates to the level of the waist.

**3.** The third zone cuts across the talus on the sole of the foot and the lower tibia (the larger bone of the lower leg) on the upper part of the foot and is equivalent to an imaginary line between the two ankle bones (malleoli). It relates to the level of the pelvic floor.

These transverse zones in the feet form a grid-like pattern with the longitudinal zones.

- The area above the level of the shoulder girdle, covering all the phalanges, relates to the head and neck areas – those areas found in the body above the level of the shoulder girdle.

- The area between the shoulder girdle and the level of the waist, covering the metatarsals, relates to the parts of the body found in the thorax and upper abdomen (between shoulder girdle and waist level).

- The area below waist level, over the tarsals, corresponds to the abdomen and pelvis.

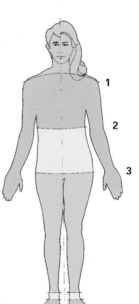

An additional transverse zone, though not described by Hanne Marquardt, relates to the level of the diaphragm. On the foot this level is found just below the ball, an area across the foot below the head of the first metatarsal. The diaphragm level is a very useful area in helping to determine the position of reflex areas, since there are a number of parts of the body situated between the diaphragm and the waist, and therefore the corresponding reflex areas are found in the feet between the levels of the diaphragm and the waist.

With an understanding of where all the different body parts are in terms of the longitudinal and transverse zones, reflex areas can then be identified in the same zones of the feet.

# Foot Structure

Each foot is made up of twenty-six bones: phalanges (toe bones), metatarsals and tarsals. There are fourteen phalanges: each toe has three except for the big toe which has only two. In line with each toe, next to the phalanges, are the five metatarsal bones. Then there are seven tarsal bones – five smaller ones called the medial, intermediate and lateral cuneiform bones, the navicular bone and the cuboid bone, and two larger ones called the talus and the calcaneum (the heel bone).

## UPPER ASPECT OF THE BONES OF THE FOOT

1. proximal phalanx of fifth toe

2. cuneiforms

3. base of fifth metatarsal

4. cuboid

5. navicular

6. neck of talus

7. sustentaculum tali

8. surface for medial malleolus

9. surface for lateral malleolus

10. surface for tibia

11. posterior tubercle

12. calcaneum

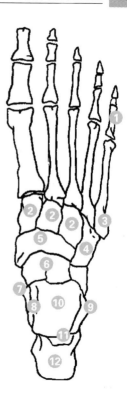

# POSITIONS OF THE REFLEX AREAS

## The Sole of the Foot

Most parts of the body are represented in the soles of the feet, with those parts found on the right side of the body represented in the right foot and those found on the left side of the body represented in the left foot. The positioning of the reflex areas is as listed below.

### REFLEX AREAS OF THE SOLES OF THE FEET

**1**. Neck **2**. Top of head and brain **3**. Pituitary **4**. Side of head and brain **5**. Sinuses **6**. Eyes **7**. Eustachian tubes **8**. Ears **9**. Thyroid **10**. Parathyroids **11**. Shoulders **12**. Trachea **13**. Bronchi **14**. Lungs **15**. Heart **16**. Oesophagus **17**. Diaphragm **18**. Solar plexus **19**. Spleen **20**. Liver **21**. Stomach **22**. Pancreas **23**. Gall bladder **24**. Adrenal **25**. Transverse colon **26**. Kidneys **27**. Descending colon **28**. Ascending colon **29**. Ureter tubes **30**. Small intestine **31**. Bladder **32**. Sigmoid colon **33**. Rectum **34**. Ileo-caecal valve **35**. Sciatic nerve **36**. Spine/cervical **37**. Spine/thoracic **38**. Spine/lumbar **39**. Spine/sacral **40**. Spine/coccyx

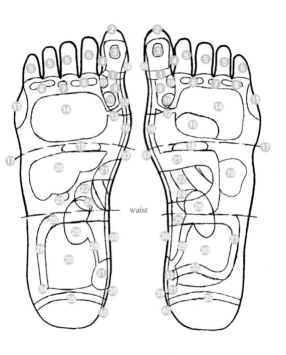

waist

# The Outer Side of the Foot

Reflex areas on the outer side of the foot relate to the arm and elbow, sacro-iliac joint, muscles of pelvis, knee, hip, ovary (in the female) / testis (in the male).

## REFLEX AREAS OF THE OUTER SIDE OF THE FOOT

1. Lymph nodes of pelvis/groin
2. Sciatic nerve/uterus/ prostate/rectum
3. Fallopian tube/vas deferens
4. Sacro-iliac
5. Ovary/testes
6. Muscles of the pelvis
7. Sciatic nerve
8. Hip
9. Knee
10. Elbow
11. Arm
12. Lymph nodes of axilla
13. Abdominal lymph
14. Breast
15. Sternum
16. Neck
17. Face
18. Ribs
19. Shoulders

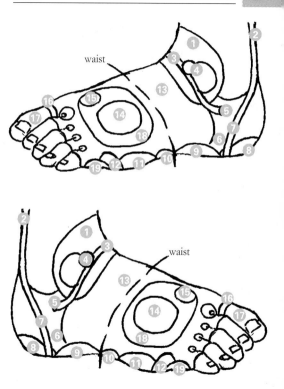

waist

waist

# The Inner Side of the Foot

Reflex areas on the inner side of the foot relate to the spine (cervical, thoracic, lumbar, sacrum, coccyx), uterus (in the female)/ prostate (in the male).

## REFLEX AREAS OF THE INNER SIDE OF THE FOOT

| | |
|---|---|
| **1.** Abdominal lymph | **11.** Lymph nodes of pelvis/groin |
| **2.** Ribs | **12.** Sciatic/uterus/ prostate/rectum |
| **3.** Breast | **13.** Bladder |
| **4.** Upper lymph nodes | **14.** Sciatic nerve |
| **5.** Teeth | **15.** Spine/coccyx |
| **6.** Lymph drainage | **16.** Sternum |
| **7.** Face | **17.** Spine/cervical |
| **8.** Neck | **18.** Spine/ thoracic |
| **9.** Uterus/ prostate | **19.** Spine/lumbar |
| **10.** Fallopian tube/ vas deferens | **20.** Spine/sacral |

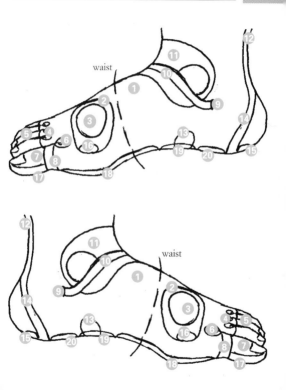

waist

waist

# The Top of the Foot

Reflex areas on the top of the foot relate to the face, teeth, fallopian tube (in the female)/ vas deferens (in the male), lymphatic system including breast.

## REFLEX AREAS OF THE TOP OF THE FOOT

| | |
|---|---|
| **1.** Face | **13.** Fallopian tube/ |
| **2.** Neck | vas deferens |
| **3.** Teeth | **14.** Lymph nodes of |
| **4.** Upper lymph nodes | pelvis/groin |
| **5.** Shoulder | **15.** Knee |
| **6.** Sternum | **16.** Hip |
| **7.** Lymph nodes of axilla | **17.** Spine/coccyx |
| **8.** Breast | **18.** Lymph drainage |
| **9.** Arm | **19.** Spine/cervical |
| **10.** Ribs | **20.** Spine/thoracic |
| **11.** Elbow | **21.** Spine/lumbar |
| **12.** Abdominal lymph | **22.** Spine/sacral |

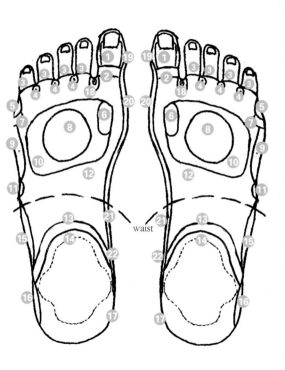

waist

# HAND REFLEXOLOGY

Although reflexology treatment is usually associated with feet, it is possible to practise reflexology on the hands. There are reflex areas for all the parts of the body in the hands just as in the feet.

For the purposes of reflexology there are two main differences between hand and foot:

- Since the hands are smaller than the feet, the reflex areas are smaller. This means they are sometimes more difficult to find precisely.

- Since the hands are used for so many different tasks their sensitivity to the massage is usually not as great as the feet which are generally protected in shoes and socks for most of the time.

The reflex areas found in the left and right feet will be found in similar areas in the left and right hands. The palm of the hand corresponds to the sole of the foot; the back of the hand to the top of the foot. Those reflex areas found on the big toe side of the foot will be found down the thumb side of the hand and those found down the outer border of the foot will be found mainly on the back of the hand. Since the longitudinal zones extend through the body, ending in the hands and the feet, the position of reflex areas in the hands will be as in the feet. The transverse zones cannot be so easily identified in the hands, but waist level lies approximately half way down the hand and therefore parts of the body above waist level will be represented in the upper part of the hand and parts below waist level in the lower part of the hand.

A similar technique is used and the same order of treatment is recommended. Since the hands are a smaller area than the feet, a full treatment will take less time than a full treatment to the feet, and the treatment time will be thirty to forty minutes.

It may be more appropriate for a reflexology practitioner to give a hand treatment than a foot treatment if:

- The foot is damaged
- The foot is absent
- The feet are extremely ticklish.

Treatment may be given to one foot and one hand or to both hands instead of the feet.

The hands are more accessible for self treatment and can be used for a full treatment (which is preferable) or for working just a few areas in order to relieve symptoms such as headaches or backaches.

# Reflexology Areas of the Left Hand

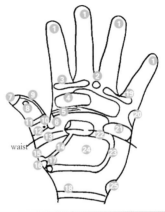

waist

| | | |
|---|---|---|
| **1.** Sinuses | **10.** Parathyroids | **18.** Sciatic |
| **2.** Eustachian tube | **11.** Neck | **19.** Ear |
| **3.** Eye | **12.** Thyroid | **20.** Shoulder |
| **4.** Heart | **13.** Pancreas/ | **21.** Spleen |
| **5.** Solar plexus | stomach | **22.** Transverse colon |
| **6.** Lymph drainage | **14.** Ureter tube | **23.** Descending |
| **7.** Top of head/brain | **15.** Bladder | colon |
| **8.** Pituitary | **16.** Uterus/ prostate | **24.** Small intestine |
| **9.** Side of head/ brain | **17.** Rectum | **25.** Ovary/testes |

# Reflexology Areas of the Right Hand

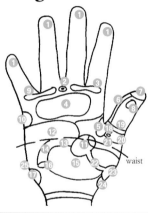

waist

1. Sinuses
2. Eustachian tube
3. Eye
4. Lung
5. Lymph drainage
6. Side of head/ brain
7. Top of head/ brain
8. Pituitary
9. Ear
10. Shoulder
11. Adrenal/kidney
12. Liver
13. Transverse colon
14. Ascending colon
15. Small intestine
16. Ileo-caecal valve
17. Ovary/testes
18. Parathyroid
19. Neck
20. Thyroid
21. Stomach
22. Ureter tube
23. Bladder
24. Uterus /prostate
25. Sciatic

# How to Give Treatment

When you first visit a reflexologist, the practitioner will take a detailed medical history in order to make sure that it is safe to go ahead with treatment and to plan the appropriate course of action.

Patients will then remove their shoes and socks and be seated in a recliner chair or similar so that they are in a relaxed position with the neck and back supported and the legs raised to a comfortable height for treatment. In order for the feet to be as relaxed as possible it is important for the knees to be slightly bent and for the lower leg, from knee to ankle, to be totally supported. A pillow or cushion covered with a towel will be placed under the feet.

For self treatment, the position may not be so comfortable and relaxing. However, it is important to sit as comfortably as possible with the back well supported, and you will need to bend the knee so that the foot is in reach and to rest the foot on a cushion for support. Ensure that you are in a quiet environment to benefit fully from treatment.

# Evaluating the Foot

Before treatment the feet will be examined, as a number of observations can be made from their feel and appearance.

## TEMPERATURE OF THE FEET

On first touching the feet you will notice their temperature. If they are very cold or hot then this may be linked to problems in the body. First consideration must be given to factors such as the outside temperature (you would expect feet to be hot on a very hot day or cold on a very cold day), and footwear (wearing open sandals without socks or stockings on a very cold day will make the feet cold, wearing synthetic fibres is more likely to make them sweat). If the feet are cold this suggests poor circulation, which may also be present in other areas, affecting the proper functioning of other parts of the body. If feet are hot and perspiring there could be a glandular imbalance.

# SKIN CONDITION AND COLOUR OF THE FEET

The skin condition may be significant. Look out for the following:

- Dry skin is sometimes an indication of poor circulation, a glandular imbalance or even an allergy.

- The colour of the skin may also indicate imbalances in the body. Areas of redness or blueness indicate poor circulation, though small areas of redness may be due to a shoe rubbing the foot.

- Where there are corns and callouses, these may form on a part of the foot relating to an imbalance in the corresponding part of the body. The same may be true of infections such as verrucae.

- Other conditions to look for include athlete's foot, which is a fungal infection often found between the toes and below the toes on the sole of the foot. This could relate to an eye or ear problem.

- An ingrowing toe-nail, particularly on the big toe, may relate to headaches.

- Blisters and scars on the foot may relate to a problem in the corresponding part of the body, and puffiness may relate to puffiness or swelling in the corresponding part of the body.

If there is an area of infection in the foot then this area should be covered so that the practitioner does not directly contact that infection. Another, surer way for the practitioner to avoid picking up infection is for the hand to be worked on instead.

## BONE STRUCTURE OF THE FEET

Structural problems with the feet can indicate problems in the corresponding part of the body.

Examples could include:

- Flat feet, where the inner arch of the foot is dropped and which may then suggest a problem with the spine.
- Hammer toes or other toe deformities, which may relate to problems in the head, sinus or teeth areas.
- Bunions forming on the inner side of the big toe, which may relate to neck problems or thyroid imbalances.
- Injury around the ankle bones, which may point to problems in the pelvic region.

## MUSCLE TONE OF THE FEET

On first touching the feet, their overall muscle tone is felt and if the feet are very tense then there is probably tension throughout the body. If the feet feel rather lacking in muscle tone, then there is probably poor muscle tone throughout the body. An area that feels tight will suggest tightness in the corresponding part of the body – this is sometimes found in the large intestine area when constipation is present or in the hip area if there is stiffness in this region. If an area feels slack when worked on then this will suggest a lack of muscle tone in the corresponding part of the body.

## TISSUE STRUCTURE OF THE FEET

If there is oedema or lymph congestion in an area of the foot there may be congestion in the corresponding part of the body. This is often found over and around the ankles, where it may relate to congestion in the pelvic region.

It is not always possible to say if the problem in the foot is the cause or effect of the problem in the corresponding part of the body. However, while there is not always a relationship between the foot problem and a problem in the body, the above factors should always be considered.

In some areas of the feet, 'grittiness' or 'scrunchiness' may be felt when pressure is applied. It is thought that this comes from crystalline deposits of either calcium or lactic acid which settle in the nerve endings. These 'gritty' areas relate to imbalances in the corresponding part of the body, but massage may well disperse the deposits, unblocking congestion in that area.

# Technique

- The way that treatment is given does vary from one practitioner to another, since different training schools tend to teach different techniques. The method to be described is one employed by many practitioners with good results and is quite easy to apply.

- Massage to the reflex areas is given mainly using the thumb, though in some instances it is easier to use finger pressure. It is very important that the thumb and finger nails are kept short in order to avoid pressing the nail onto the reflex areas and causing discomfort.

- With the thumb held bent, the fleshy part near to the tip and slightly to the side of the thumb should be applied to the reflex area without pressing the nail into the foot. The pressure is held on the point for a moment or so and then released, although the thumb stays bent. The thumb is then lifted just off the point and then pressed onto the next reflex point.

- Within each reflex area there will be a number of reflex points, each only about the size of a pinhead. When working a specific reflex area, all the reflex points within the area must be treated, so the massage applied must be very precise in order to reach all the reflex points.

- The hand not applying the massage is used to support the area being worked on, usually on the opposite side of the foot. When working any area in the upper part of the foot above the level of the diaphragm, the toes must always be supported.

- The pressure used should be such that the practitioner does not feel that they are having to strain to exert it. Another technique that is sometimes used to apply the massage involves bending and straightening of the thumb joint when moving from one reflex point to the next. Although many use this technique, which involves a much quicker action, it is felt that this procedure puts considerable strain on the thumb joint, which might result in damage to this joint after many years of practice.

- Once the correct technique has been learnt, the hands should be as relaxed as possible when applying the massage so as to avoid injury to their joints.

# What the Patient Will Feel

When pressure is applied to the different reflex areas in the foot the patient should be aware of its effect but it should not feel uncomfortable. Within the acceptable range of pressures used to give treatment, some practitioners will be applying pressure at the lighter end of the acceptable scale and some at the heavier end. From the patient angle, some will prefer a lighter pressure, some a heavier pressure. This will be an individual matter to be worked out between practitioner and patient.

Apart from being aware of a pressure being applied to the different reflex areas, in some areas a degree of discomfort may be felt by the patient. This discomfort will relate to an imbalance in the corresponding part of the body. Some areas may feel just slightly painful when pressure is applied, and in some areas it may be more painful. The more painful an area is then the more out of balance the corresponding part of the body may be. However, it must be stressed that the treatment should never really hurt. The pain felt in a reflex area is short-term and will disappear once pressure is released. When an area is very painful the pressure will be eased off but the thumb still held over the point and eased away gently until the pain reduces.

# What a Treatment Session Involves

## CLEAN FEET

Once a medical history has been taken and the feet have been examined, treatment can begin. Often people think that the practice of reflexology must be an unpleasant experience, since the feet can often be rather sweaty and dirty. It is hoped that anyone presenting themselves for treatment will have ensured that their feet are in a reasonable state, but should the feet be a bit dirty or moist then either the person should be asked to go and wash them or the feet could be wiped over with a wet wipe.

A small amount of talcum powder will then be massaged onto the feet. Talc is the best medium to work with, since it will absorb any excess moisture and will also smooth over any rough areas if the skin tends to be dry. It also allows the technique to be applied more easily. It is not essential to use talc but it is usually preferred. It is not appropriate to use an oil on the feet, since this will make the skin surface too slippery and the resultant sliding between reflex points will make the treatment less precise.

## FULL TREATMENT

In order to achieve the best results and treat the whole body, massage will be given to all the reflexes of the feet following the order of treatment. All of the right foot will be worked on, followed by all of the left foot. As treatment proceeds, the patient should be encouraged to give feedback on what is being felt. It is particularly important to find out which reflexes are tender. With experience of giving treatment, differences in the feet may be felt, but this is possible only when many pairs of feet have been treated.

## EXTRA ATTENTION TO IMPORTANT REFLEX AREAS

Although all the reflexes should be massaged in a full treatment, some are more important than others. On completing the treatment, extra massage can be given to the important reflex areas. This involves returning to certain areas and repeating the massage once or twice. If there are many different conditions present and they cannot all be reworked, the most important will have to be isolated.

## LENGTH OF TREATMENT

A full treatment session will take about one hour, of which the actual length of time required to massage all of the reflex areas should come to about forty-five to fifty minutes. If the treatment takes less time then it suggests that the reflex areas will not have been massaged as thoroughly as they should have been. If treatment takes more time then there is always the risk of overworking and the possibility that excessive reactions might occur. The number of reflex areas requiring extra attention will also affect the length of time that treatment takes, but an hour is quite enough.

Normally treatment will be given once a week, since this allows the body a chance, in the meantime, to start returning to a balanced state. An average course of treatment involves three to six sessions at weekly intervals, though if improvement is marked the interval might be extended towards the end of a course of treatment to once a fortnight. Once the body has been brought back into balance and conditions cleared this improvement should last, but many people who have had a successful course of treatment decide to make regular visits perhaps once every four or six weeks in order to maintain their level of improved health and prevent other problems occurring. This is a sensible approach – you do not need to be unwell to receive reflexology treatment.

# GENERAL ADVICE

Reflexology is in many ways a very simple form of therapy involving massage to areas of the feet to bring about healing reactions in the body. If treatment is given correctly then no ill-effects should occur, but it is a very powerful method and it is possible to do harm if administered incorrectly. The main considerations should be :

- Do not overtax any area by working for too long, too often or with too heavy a pressure. This might cause a person to feel unwell and also produce imbalances in the body which although probably not irreversible are certainly unnecessary.

- Do not diagnose medical conditions or advise on altering medication. It is possible to detect areas of the body which are out of balance and therefore show as tender reflex areas in the feet, but this does not indicate the exact nature of the imbalance, and any problem that persists should always be investigated by the patient's doctor.

There are very few occasions when it is not appropriate to give treatment, but there are some, and these should be noted.

# Contraindications

It is inappropriate to give reflexology treatment in the following situations:

### ACUTE INFECTIOUS DISEASE

In this case there is obviously the risk of catching the disease.

### FEVERS, VERY HIGH TEMPERATURES

Again there is the risk of catching an infection which is causing the fever or high temperature, and also in the acute stage of these types of illness it is better to let nature take its course in trying to fight the fever. By giving reflexology treatment additional toxins might be released into the system which would overload it more.

### DEEP VEIN THROMBOSIS OR PHLEBITIS

With a deep vein thrombosis, usually present in the leg, there is a blood clot present and there is always the risk that this might spread to another part of the body and cause a more serious effect, such as moving to the brain and inducing a stroke. With phlebitis where there is inflammation of a vein, there is always a risk of a thrombosis developing. Although it is unlikely that reflexology would cause a clot to move it is best to err on the side of caution and not treat anyone suffering from these conditions. Once the condition has cleared treatment can be given.

## RISK PREGNANCY

For a woman who has never received reflexology treatment and who is enjoying a first pregnancy, or who has had a previous miscarriage, it is probably best not to give treatment, particularly in the early months of the pregnancy. It is better for the body to adjust to the new situation and it also rules out blame being assigned to the treatment should a miscarriage occur at this time.

## SEVERE OSTEOPOROSIS

In the case of severe osteoporosis, the bones become very brittle and any slight pressure may cause a fracture. If the condition involves the feet, then it might be damaging to work over the bones of the foot.

## DIRECTLY AFTER REPLACEMENT SURGERY

After replacement surgery involving parts such as a new hip joint, new heart valve or new pacemaker to the heart, there will always be a possibility of rejection of that new part. Therefore it is best to avoid a far-reaching treatment such as reflexology until it is considered that this risk has passed.

Extra care should always be taken in the following situations:

## HEART CONDITIONS

With any person who has a heart condition, extra care should be taken in order not to overstimulate the heart, which may already be under strain.

## EPILEPSY

In some instances those who are epileptic find that they have a fit following treatment. This is by no means always the case, and many epileptics have found treatment helpful in reducing the number of fits which they experience, but because of this risk an epileptic patient should always be warned of the possibility and extra care taken, particularly when working the reflex areas to the head and brain.

## FOOT PROBLEMS

There may be some instances when working directly on the feet might aggravate a foot problem that is present. This can sometimes be the case with arthritis in the feet, gout in the big toe or osteoporosis, where yet more pain could be experienced if the affected joints are worked on directly. Nor is it appropriate to work directly over varicose veins in the feet which might then become further inflamed.

## PREGNANCY

When a woman is pregnant extra care should always be taken, particularly when treating the reflex area to the uterus, so as not to aggravate the pregnancy in any way.

## PROSTHESES

These are parts which are foreign to the body and there is always a risk that the body might reject them. They could include such things as contact lenses, replacement hips and knees, and metal pins and plates in broken bones. It is possible to treat people with these 'artificial' parts, but with initial caution in case the treatment should detect the part as unnatural to the body. It is quite common for people who wear contact lenses to find that when receiving treatment the eyes become quite uncomfortable and that they are best advised to take their lenses out before treatment, though this is not always the case.

## MEDICATION

Conditions where medication is being taken where it might be necessary for the medication to be adjusted include:

• High blood pressure

• Diabetes

• Underactive thyroid

In these cases, the reflexology treatment will be working in a similar way to the medication – by, for example, trying to lower the blood pressure, helping the pancreas produce more of the hormone insulin or helping the thyroid produce more of the hormone thyroxine. Hence it is important that the patient is aware of how the treatment may work, in order that they, or their doctor, can monitor their medication requirements.

Medication which might mask the sensitivity of the reflex areas includes:

- painkillers
- tranquillisers
- anti-depressants

These may cause the patient not to feel tender areas in the feet, which might encourage the practitioner to overwork an area.

Reflexology treatment should always be given with care, but especially in the cases mentioned above. Remember that the reactions of one person to treatment can be different from those of another person with the same condition and also that people may respond differently to treatment received from different practitioners. Provided treatment is given with care and understanding of the correct procedures then there is little risk of any harm being done.

# THE COMPLETE TREATMENT

To give a full treatment it is recommended that an orderly procedure is followed. If this order is always observed, it will ensure that all the parts of the feet are worked on and all parts of the body are treated. Although there are different approaches to treatment, the suggested order given below (which runs, giving an introduction to each body part, on left-hand pages, through thirty-eight stages) is considered sound and has been found to achieve good results. It is the order taught by The Bayly School of Reflexology. Treatment is given first to the right foot and, when this is completed, to the left. After completing all of the areas in the right foot a few exercises are given to the foot before commencing work on the left foot. At the very end of a full treatment to both feet, the solar plexus breathing exercise is carried out. For self treatment it may be necessary to alter the technique slightly, since it may be easier to use the opposite hand to that suggested.

Running alongside each stage of the Complete Treatment, on each right-hand page, is a foot chart showing the precise locations of the reflex area for that part of the body.

# A Recommended Order of Treatment

## RIGHT FOOT

1. Pituitary
2. Neck
3. Side of head/brain
4. Top of head/brain
5. Spine (cervical, thoracic, lumbar, sacrum, coccyx)
6. Face
7. Sinuses
8. Teeth
9. Eye
10. Eustachian tube
11. Ear
12. Shoulder
13. Arm and elbow
14. Thyroid and parathyroids
15. Lung
16. Solar plexus
17. Liver and gall bladder
18. Stomach
19. Pancreas
20. Small intestine
21. Large intestine (ileo-caecal valve, ascending colon, transverse colon)
22. Bladder
23. Ureter tube
24. Kidney
25. Adrenal gland
26. Sciatic nerve (+ up the back of the leg)

**27.** Sacro-iliac joint

**28.** Muscles of the pelvis

**29.** Knee

**30.** Hip

**31.** Ovary/Testis

**32.** Fallopian tubes and vas deferens

**33.** Uterus and prostate gland

**34.** Lymphatic system (including the breast)

**35.** Lymphatic drainage

## EXERCISES

**E1** Rotation of toes

**E2** 'Wringing' of foot

**E3** 'Kneading' of foot

**E4** Rotation of ankle

## LEFT FOOT

Follow the same order as for the right foot but include:

**15b.** Heart

**17b.** Spleen

**21b.** Large intestine (transverse colon, descending colon, sigmoid colon, rectum)

## EXERCISE

**E5** Solar plexus breathing (both feet together at very end of treatment)

# RIGHT FOOT

## ① Pituitary

The pituitary gland is a hormonal gland the size of a pea found in the centre of the brain. It is often known as the master gland of the body, since it controls the actions of many of the other hormonal glands including the thyroid gland, the adrenal glands and the reproductive glands. It also influences kidney function and growth.

### TREATMENT

*Using the right thumb apply pressure to the centre of the big toe; use the left hand to support the top of the toe. Having worked the very centre of the big toe then work a small square area all round the centre point and this will relate to other parts in the centre of the brain.*

## REFLEXOLOGY AREA

The reflex areas for the pituitary gland are found in both feet in the centre of the pad of the big toe.

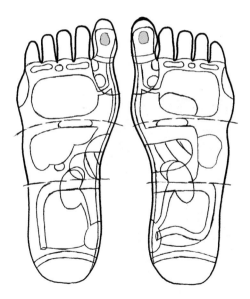

# 2 Neck

The neck connects the head to the body, and in the back of the neck are various muscles which support the head to keep it upright. Not only can supporting the head cause great strain on those muscles, but problems in the back are sometimes transferred to the neck and felt in the form of tension there.

## TREATMENT

*Using the right thumb start on the inner border of the foot and work across just above where the big toe joins the foot*

## REFLEXOLOGY AREA

The reflex areas for the neck (back of neck) are found in
both feet at the base of the big toe just above where it
joins the foot.

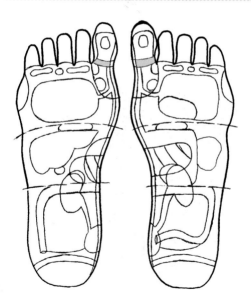

# 3 Side of the Head and Side of the Brain

The side of the head includes the scalp, hair and skull. The regions of the brain found here include important regions for hearing and smelling. This area also encompasses the muscles to the side of the head and neck, which can often become tense.

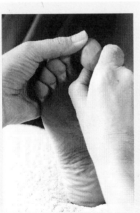

## TREATMENT

*Using the right thumb work up the side of the big toe, next to the second toe, from the base of the toe to the tip.*

## REFLEXOLOGY AREA

The reflex areas for the side of the head and the side of the brain are found in both feet up the side (adjacent to the second toe) of the big toe.

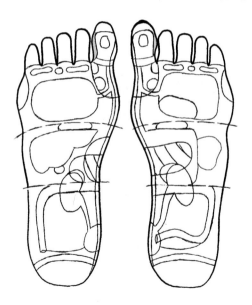

# ④ Top of the Head and Top of the Brain

The top of the head includes the scalp, hair and skull. The regions of the brain found here include areas which control muscles and interpret sensations. Headaches involving pain at the front of the head are often the result of problems in this area.

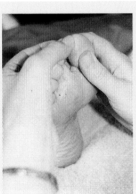

### TREATMENT

*Using the left thumb work over the top of the big toe from the second toe side to the inner side.*

## REFLEXOLOGY AREA

The reflex areas for the top of the head and the top of the brain are found in both feet across the top of the big toe.

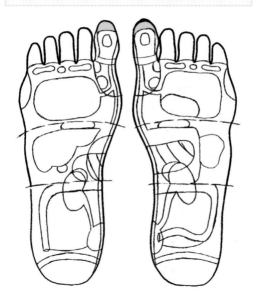

# 5 Spine

The spine is made up of bony segments called vertebrae, and these can be divided into five regions. The uppermost region is made up of the seven cervical vertebrae, followed by the twelve thoracic vertebrae, the five lumbar vertebrae, the sacrum and the coccyx. The spine surrounds the spinal cord, which is the nerve link between the brain and the rest

## TREATMENT

**(5a)** *Using the left thumb work down the inner side of the foot following the bony arch of the foot. Start along the side of the big toe (cervical spine) right down to just in front of the heel (coccyx reflex).*

## REFLEXOLOGY AREA

The reflex areas for the spine are found in both feet all along the inner margin of the foot following the bony arch of the foot. The cervical region lies along the big toe, then come the thoracic region and lumbar region, followed by the sacrum and then the coccyx, which is found just in front of the back of the heel.

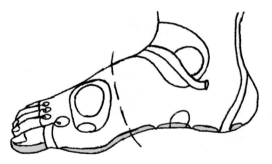

of the body, so the reflex area will relate to both the spinal bones and nerves. Some movement is possible between the individual bones, particularly in the cervical and lumbar regions, making these the most likely to develop problems. Between bones are invertebral discs, which can become worn, causing pressure on the nerves.

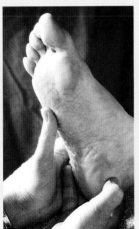

**(5b)** *Having worked down the spine reflex, change hands and come back up the spine reflex using the right thumb following a slightly straighter line up the side of the foot. As you work back up the spine, rest the fingers of the right hand underneath the back of the heel to start with, then when you get to about waist level bring the fingers of the right hand round to rest on the top of the foot.*

## REFLEXOLOGY AREA

The reflex area for the spine is found along the inner side of the foot.

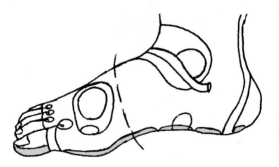

# 6 Face

The face is made up of many muscles. This means that it can suffer from a build-up of tension in the same way as any other area of the body. The reflex area also relates to the skin of the face.

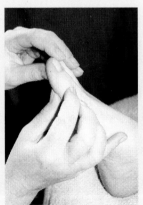

## TREATMENT

*Use finger pressure to work the area on the front of the big toe from the base of the toe to just below the nail.*

## REFLEXOLOGY AREA

The reflex areas for the face are found in both feet on the upper aspect of the big toe, the upper aspect of the base of the big toe contains the reflex area to the front of the neck and the throat.

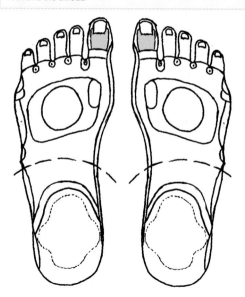

# 7 Sinuses

The sinuses are air-filled cavities found in the skull behind the eyebrows, above and to the sides of the nose and below the eyes in the bones of the skull. They help reduce the weight of the head. They link with the nose and are lined by mucus-producing cells.

## TREATMENT

**(7a)** *Using the right thumb work from the base of the toe to the tip. Then work up the sides of the toes on both inner and outer borders of the toe.*

**(7b)** *Each toe has to be worked on in turn. Throughout this treatment, make sure that the toe is being supported from behind using the left hand.*

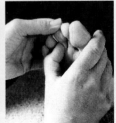

## REFLEXOLOGY AREA

The reflex areas for the sinuses are found in both feet up the backs and sides of the second, third, fourth and fifth toes.

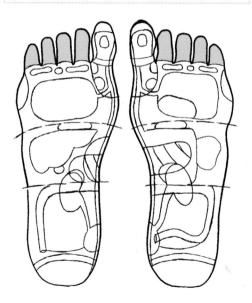

# 8 Teeth

In the adult there are thirty-two teeth in the mouth arranged in an upper and lower row with equal pairs of teeth on both sides – the incisors, canines, pre-molars, molars and wisdom teeth. The teeth begin the process of digesting food, and this reflex area also helps with mouth and gum problems.

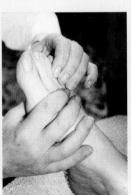

## TREATMENT

*Using finger pressure, work the fronts of toes from the base up to just below the nail.*

## REFLEXOLOGY AREA

The reflex areas for the teeth and also the gums are found in both feet on the upper aspects of the second, third, fourth and fifth toes.

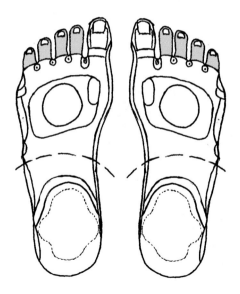

# 9 Eyes

The two eyes are the organs for sight and are situated within the orbital cavities in the front of the skull. The light rays pass through the lens of the eye to the back of the eye, from where messages are sent by nerves to the regions of the brain responsible for vision. Apart from the usual diseases associated with the eye, people may suffer from eyestrain, which causes headaches.

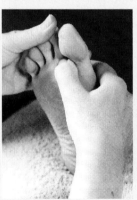

## TREATMENT

*Using the right thumb, work just below where the second and third toes join the sole of the foot across from beneath the second toe to beneath the third toe. Use the left hand to straighten and pull back the toes slightly.*

## REFLEXOLOGY AREA

The reflex areas for the eyes are found in both feet just below where the second and third toes join the foot.

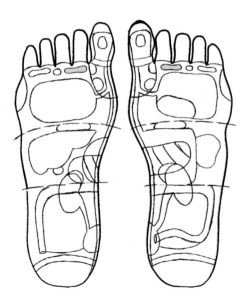

# 10 Eustachian Tubes

The Eustachian tubes connect the middle ear to the throat and are responsible for maintaining equal pressure on either side of the ear drum, which is necessary for correct hearing. A person's awareness of these tubes may be heightened when they have a cold, or when flying, when the tubes become blocked due to pressure.

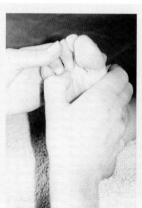

## TREATMENT

*Use the right thumb to work just below the web between the third and fourth toe on the sole of the foot.*

## REFLEXOLOGY AREA

The reflex areas for the Eustachian tubes are found in
both feet just below the web between the third and
fourth toe.

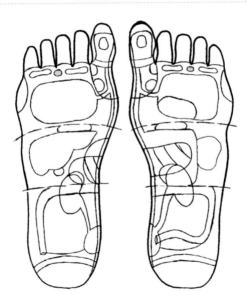

# 11 Ears

The two ears are the organs of hearing and are also important for balance. The outer ear leads down to the ear drum, and in the middle ear are three small bones which are involved in the process of hearing. The inner ear contains the receptors for hearing and balance, and nerves from these areas pass to the regions of the brain responsible for hearing and balance.

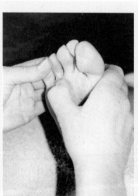

## TREATMENT

*Using the right thumb, work just below where the fourth and fifth toes join the sole of the foot across from beneath the fourth toe to beneath the fifth toe. Use the left hand to straighten and pull back the toes slightly.*

## REFLEXOLOGY AREA

The reflex areas for the ears are found in both feet just below where the fourth and fifth toes join the foot.

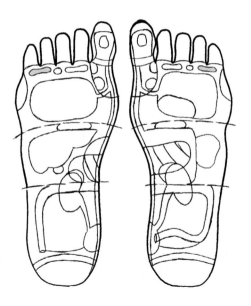

# 12 Shoulder

The shoulder joint is where the arm attaches to the upper body. This is a ball and socket joint, with the head of the humerus (the bone of the upper arm) sitting in a socket to the outer side of the shoulder girdle.

## TREATMENT

*Using the left thumb, work the area on the sole of the foot beneath the little toe and on the top of the foot.*

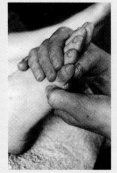

## REFLEXOLOGY AREA

The reflex areas for the shoulder joints are found just below the base of the little toe on the sole of the foot and also in a similar area on the outer side of the foot and on the top of the foot.

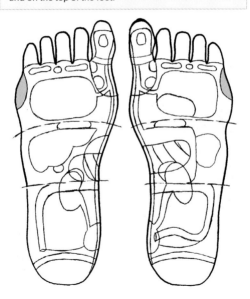

# 13 Arm and Elbow

The two arms are the upper limbs, with the upper arm connected to the body via the shoulder joint and the lower arm (the forearm) attached to the hand at the wrist joint. One affliction which is becoming more and more common, due to people's increased use of computer keyboards, is Repetitive Strain Injury (RSI).

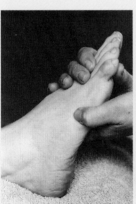

## TREATMENT

**(13a)** *Using the left thumb, work down the outer border of the foot from the shoulder reflex to the bony projection about halfway down the foot. This area relates to the arm and the bony projection to the elbow.*

## REFLEXOLOGY AREA

The reflex areas for the arms are found in both feet on the outer margin from the base of the little toe extending down to the bony projection about halfway down the outer margin of the foot. The reflex areas for the elbow are found in both feet over the bony projection (the cuboid notch) about halfway down the outer margin of the foot.

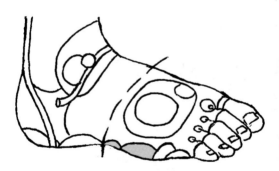

The elbow is the point at which the upper arm bone (technically known as the 'humerus') joins the lower arm bones (the 'radius' and 'ulna' respectively). Together, these three bones form a hinge joint, which – unlike the ball and socket joint of the hip – allows movement in only one direction.

**(13b-13c)** *Work back up the same area using the left hand.*

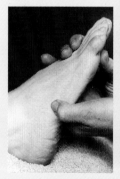

## REFLEXOLOGY AREA

The reflex areas for the upper and lower limbs are found along the outer side of the foot.

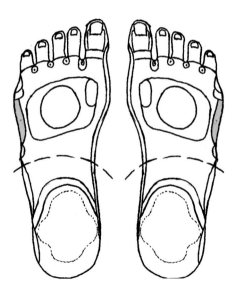

# 14 Thyroid and Parathyroids

The thyroid gland is found in the front of the lower part of the neck. It produces hormones which influence the metabolic rate in the body and also the calcium levels in the blood.

## TREATMENT

**(14a)** *Using the right thumb start on the inner side of the foot working tight in beneath the ball of the big toe and then up the side of the ball of the big toe to just below the web between the first and second toe. As you work this area you will overlap the lower parathyroid reflex just as you turn the corner to come up the side of the ball of the big toe and the upper parathyroid reflex below the web between first and second toe.*

## REFLEXOLOGY AREA

The reflex areas for the thyroid are found in both feet in the upper part of the ball (metatarsal joint) of the big toe.

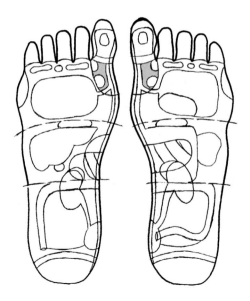

The parathyroids are four small glands situated in the back of the thyroid gland and they produce a hormone which influences the level of calcium in the blood, working in an opposite way to the hormone from the thyroid.

**(14b–14c)** *Using that same 'L'-shaped pattern cover the whole area over the pad of the big toe, which all relates to the thyroid gland.*

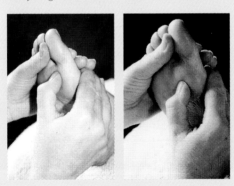

## REFLEXOLOGY AREA

The reflex areas for the parathyroids are found in both feet on the outer margins of the thyroid area in the upper part of the ball of the big toe with an upper and a lower reflex on each foot.

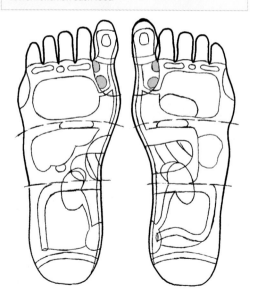

# 15 Lung

The air breathed in by the lungs takes in oxygen to the body, and that breathed out contains carbon dioxide. They have a tree-like structure with the trunk – the 'trachea' (windpipe) – dividing into two branches (or 'bronchi') which divide into 'bronchioles'. Gas exchange occurs through air sacs ('alveoli') at the end of branches.

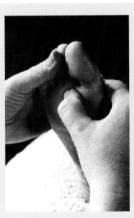

## TREATMENT

*Start in longitudinal zone 2 below the second toe and work straight across all zones using the right thumb. When you reach longitudinal zone 5, change hands and come back with the left thumb across all zones. Keep working across the ball of the foot, changing hands as you get to the side of the foot until you have worked all the area relating to the lungs.*

## REFLEXOLOGY AREA

The reflex areas for the lungs are found in both feet in the area over the ball of the foot in longitudinal zones 2, 3, 4 and 5.

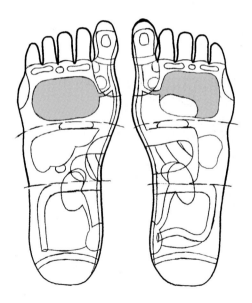

# 16 Solar Plexus

The solar plexus is a network of nerves situated just behind the diaphragm which gives off many nerve branches to supply parts of the abdomen. It is part of the nervous system in the body and is associated with breathing and relaxation. A severe blow to the solar plexus can cause loss of consciousness.

## TREATMENT

*Using the left or right thumb, work the area in zones 2 and 3 just below diaphragm level. This level corresponds to the arch of the foot, and there is sometimes quite a marked coloration change between the pinker area of the ball of the foot and the very pale skin of the rest of it.*

## REFLEXOLOGY AREA

The reflex areas for the solar plexus are found in both feet in longitudinal zones 2 and 3 just below diaphragm level.

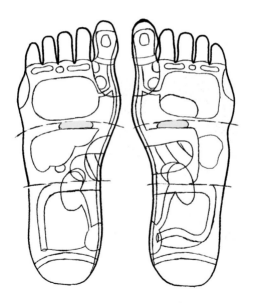

# 17 Liver and Gall Bladder

The liver is situated on the right side of the body below the diaphragm. It is a large organ and performs a number of functions including the metabolism of food substances (it can make certain proteins and store glucose as an energy reserve), the manufacture of bile, the breakdown of alcohol, the storage of some vitamins and the detoxifying of substances that might harm the body.

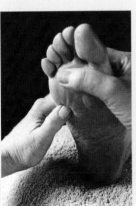

## TREATMENT

**(17a)** *Using the left thumb, start in zone 5 just below diaphragm level and work across all of the zones, then change hands when you get to the inner border of the foot and use the right thumb to come back across the zones, following a slightly lower line across the foot.*

## REFLEXOLOGY AREA

The reflex area for the liver is found in the right foot in all 5 zones just below diaphragm level and tapering off to longitudinal zones 3, 4 and 5 just above waist level.

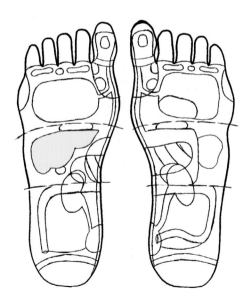

The gall bladder is attached to the lower margin of the liver, so it is found just above waist level on the right side of the body. The function of the gall bladder is to store the bile made in the liver. When foods containing fat are eaten, the bile is released down the bile duct to the small intestine. There it helps to digest the fats.

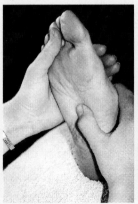

**(17b)** *Repeat these movements for the rest of the liver area, but not working so far over on the inner side of the foot with each movement, as the lower part of the liver reflex lies only in zones 5, 4 and 3.*

*As you work the lower part of the liver area you will overlap the gall bladder reflex in zone 3 just above waist level.*

## REFLEXOLOGY AREA

The reflex area for the gall bladder is found in the right foot in longitudinal zone 3 just above waist level.

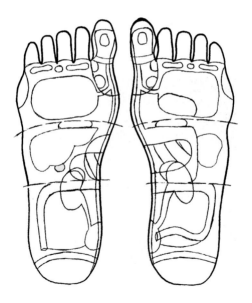

# 18 Stomach

The stomach is found in the upper abdomen mainly on the left side but reaching slightly across to the right side. It is part of the digestive system and food reaching the stomach is stored there for a few hours and mixed with gastric juices which begin the digestive process.

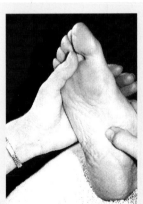

## TREATMENT

*Using the right thumb work across zone 1 just below diaphragm level. Repeat this movement a little lower down the foot each time until just above waist level.*

## REFLEXOLOGY AREA

The reflex areas for the stomach are found in both feet between diaphragm and waist level in longitudinal zones 1, 2 and 3 on the left foot and the lower part of this area in longitudinal zone 1 on the right foot.

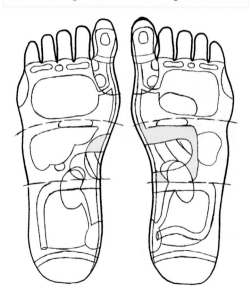

# 19 Pancreas

The pancreas is situated fairly centrally in the body just above the waist level and is overlapped by the stomach. It plays an important part in digestion by producing enzymes which travel down the pancreatic duct to the small intestine to help digest proteins, carbohydrates and fats. The pancreas also produces hormones, including insulin, which act to adjust blood sugar level.

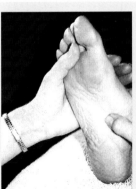

## TREATMENT

*Using the right thumb work across from zone 1 to zone 2 covering the lower half of the area between diaphragm and waist level.*

## REFLEXOLOGY AREA

The reflex areas for the pancreas are found in both feet in the lower half of the area between diaphragm and waist level in longitudinal zones 1, 2 and 3 on the left foot and zones 1 and 2 on the right foot. (It overlaps in much of this area with the reflex area for the stomach.)

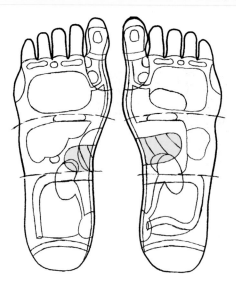

# 20 Small Intestine

The small intestine connects the stomach to the large intestine. It begins with a C-shaped area (the 'duodenum') leading to tubing which lies folded back on itself within the abdomen. The main function of the small intestine is to break down food from the stomach into particles which can be absorbed through the walls of the small intestine (through areas called 'villi') into the bloodstream.

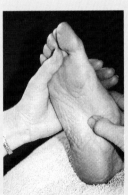

## TREATMENT

*Using the right thumb, start in zone 1 just below waist level and work across to zone 4, then change hands and use the left thumb to come back across the zones following a slightly lower line in that region. Continue similarly across the foot to just above the pad of the heel, finishing on the outer margin.*

## REFLEXOLOGY AREA

The reflex areas for the small intestines are found in both feet in the area below the waist level down to just above the heel pad in longitudinal zones 1, 2, 3 and 4.

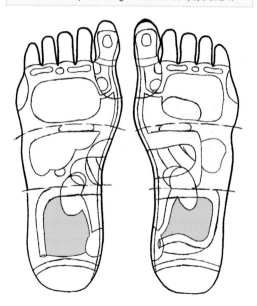

# 21 Large Intestine

(transverse colon, descending colon,
sigmoid colon, rectum)

The large intestine is a wide tube extending from the small intestine to the anus. It starts on the lower right side of the abdomen with the ileo-caecal valve. From there it passes up to waist level as the ascending colon and then stretches across waist level as the transverse colon.

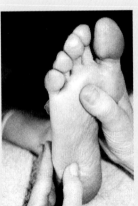

## TREATMENT

**(21a)** *Using the right thumb, work just above the pad of the heel in zones 4/5 for the ileo-caecal valve.*

## REFLEXOLOGY AREA

At waist level, the reflex area for the transverse colon starts in longitudinal zones 4 and 5 and travels across all zones in the right foot and across the left foot to longitudinal zones 4 and 5.

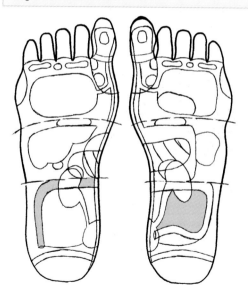

## REFLEXOLOGY AREA

The reflex areas for the large intestine are found in both feet starting with the reflex area to the ileo-caecal valve in the right foot in longitudinal zones 4 and 5 above the pad of the heel, with the reflex area to the ascending colon extending upwards from this point to waist level.

**(21b)** *Then work straight up to waist level for the ascending colon.*

**(21c)** *At waist level use the left hand to work across all the zones from 4/5 to 1 for the transverse colon.*

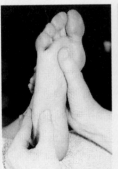
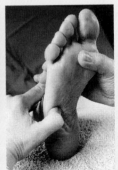

## REFLEXOLOGY AREA

The reflex area for the descending colon travels down from waist level in longitudinal zones 4 and 5 to above the pad of the heel on the left foot. The reflex area for the sigmoid colon runs back across all zones, ending in zone 1 with the reflex area for the rectum and anus.

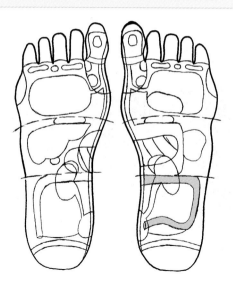

# 22 Bladder

The bladder is found in a central position in the pelvis and stores the urine produced by the kidneys until it is convenient to expel this from the body. Occasionally the bladder may suffer from infections. One of the most common of these is cystitis, which – in the main – affects women.

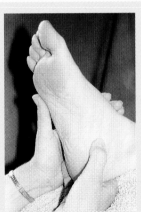

## TREATMENT

*Using the right hand, place the fingers just underneath the back of the heel so that you can get the thumb on the bladder reflex on the side of the foot. (There is sometimes a slight puffiness on the side of the foot in the position of the bladder reflex.) Work a little way on to the sole of the foot as well.*

## REFLEXOLOGY AREA

The reflex areas for the bladder are found in both feet
in longitudinal zone 1 just above the pad of the heel
and extending to an area to the inner edge of the foot,
which can often be identified as a slightly puffy area.

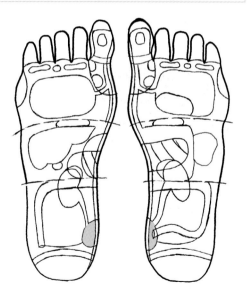

# 23 Ureter Tubes

The two ureter tubes extend, one on each side, from the kidneys at waist level down to the bladder in the pelvic cavity. These tubes are responsible for transporting urine made in the kidneys down to the bladder. From here the urine is eliminated.

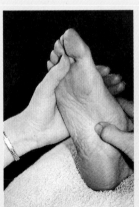

**TREATMENT**

*Using the right thumb, work upwards and outwards from the bladder area in zone 1 to zone 2 at waist level.*

## REFLEXOLOGY AREA

The reflex areas for the ureter tubes are found in both feet, extending from the kidney reflex in longitudinal zone 2 at waist level to the bladder reflex in longitudinal zone 1 just above the pad of the heel.

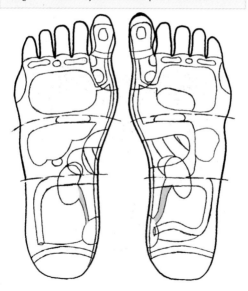

# 24 Kidney

The two kidneys are situated to the back of the body on either side of the spine at waist level and slightly above and below this level. They are important excretory organs in that they form urine, which contains waste products not required by the body, and are also important for maintaining the fluid and mineral balance in the body.

### TREATMENT

*Using the right thumb, work zones 2 and 3 at waist level and also below and above waist level.*

## REFLEXOLOGY AREA

The reflex areas for the kidneys are found in both feet in longitudinal zones 2 and 3 at waist level and a little above and below waist level.

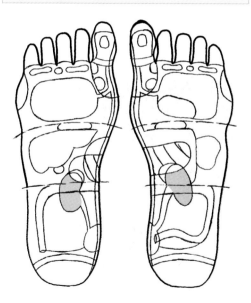

# 25 Adrenal Glands

The two adrenal glands are found just above the kidneys towards the back of the body, just above waist level. They are hormonal glands and the hormones they produce can help reduce inflammation, allergic reactions and stress. They can also help with sodium and water balance and control 'fear, flight and fight' responses. Some sex hormones are also produced by the adrenals.

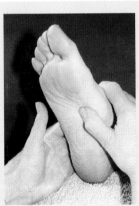

## TREATMENT

*Using the right thumbs work in zone 2 just above waist level and slightly more towards zone 1. This will be just above the kidney reflex.*

## REFLEXOLOGY AREA

The reflex areas for the adrenal glands are found in both feet in longitudinal zone 2 (the inner side nearest to zone 1) just above waist level on top of the reflex area to the kidney.

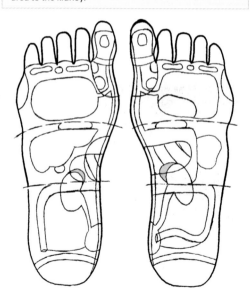

# 26 Sciatic Nerves

The sciatic nerves are the largest nerves in the body and they start near the lower spine, where lumbar and sacral nerves join together to form a sciatic nerve on each side. The nerves extend downwards across the buttock and down the back of the leg before dividing in two branches, just above the knee, which then extend down the back of the lower leg.

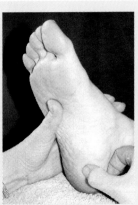

## TREATMENT

**(26a)** *Work the area a third of the way down the pad of the heel either with the right hand working from zone 1 to zone 5 or with the left hand from zone 5 to zone 1.*

## REFLEXOLOGY AREA

The reflex areas for the sciatic nerve are found in both feet across the pad of the heel.

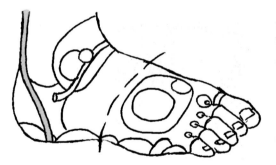

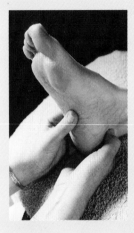

**(26b)** *Then work the rest of the area over the pad of the heel in a similar manner, which will all relate to the pelvic area. Support the foot using the palms of the hands. Continue the sciatic nerve reflex up the sides of the foot behind the ankle and up the back of the leg using the third finger of both hands on either side of the foot from where the sciatic loop ends, taking the shortest distance to the back of the heel and then up the back of the leg for about three to four inches on either side of the Achilles tendon. Then use a gentle pinching action to come down the back of the leg on either side of the Achilles tendon, place the hand under the back of the leg but without raising the leg high.*

## REFLEXOLOGY AREA

There is also a sciatic reflex up the back of each leg for a few inches on either side of the Achilles tendon.

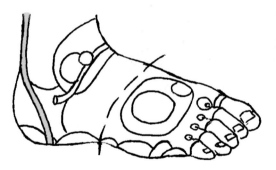

# 27 Sacro-iliac Joint

The two sacro-iliac joints are the areas where the sacrum of the spine (the area just above the tailbone) joins the ilium of the pelvis (the pelvis is a large circle of bone and the ilium is the upper part of the pelvis at the back). Thus these joints are positioned on either side of the lower spine.

## TREATMENT

*Using the left thumb, work the small dip just in front of the outer ankle bone about in line with the third toe.*

## REFLEXOLOGY AREA

The reflex areas for the sacro-iliac joints are found in both feet in a small dip just in front of the outer ankle bone about in line with the third toe.

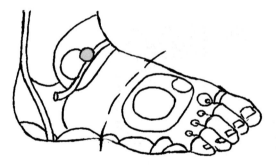

# 28 Muscles of the Pelvis

The muscles of the pelvis are those strong muscles positioned across the buttock from the sacro-iliac joint to the hip area and the top of the leg. They are often involved where there are lower back problems, or problems with the hip or leg, since walking awkwardly can strain these muscles.

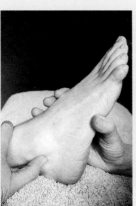

## TREATMENT

*Using the left thumb, work the area below the outer ankle bone starting at the back and moving towards the front in the area arching round beneath the outer ankle bone. Work a similar area just below this.*

## REFLEXOLOGY AREA

The reflex areas for the muscles of the pelvis are found in both feet just below the outer ankle bone.

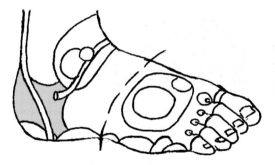

# 29 Knee

The two knee joints are where the upper and lower leg join and they are protected at the front by the knee-cap. The knee joint is a hinge joint, and many ligaments and cartilages are associated with it. The fact that knee problems are relatively common is due to the tremendous strain that knees are put under every day.

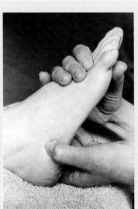

## TREATMENT

*Using the left thumb, fill in the half-moon shape from just behind the bony projection on the side of the foot to halfway towards the very back of the heel by working from the base of the foot upwards at right angles to the side of the foot.*

## REFLEXOLOGY AREA

The reflex areas for the knee are found in both feet on the outer margin of the foot in a large half-moon shape extending from the bony projection about halfway down the outer margin of the foot to halfway towards the back of the heel.

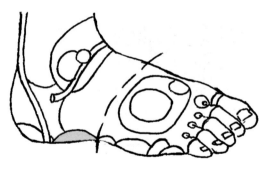

# 30 Hip

The two hip joints are where the upper leg attaches to the body through the pelvis. These are ball and socket joints, with the head of the femur (the bone of the upper leg) fitting into a socket on the outer side of the pelvic girdle. This allows movement in more than one direction, unlike hinge joints, such as those found in the knee.

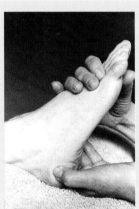

## TREATMENT

*Using the left thumb, fill in the half-moon shape from the knee reflex to the very back of the heel by working from the base of the foot upwards at right angles to the side of the foot.*

## REFLEXOLOGY AREA

The reflex areas for the hip joints are found in both feet on the outer margin of the foot in a large half-moon shape extending from the back of the heel halfway towards the bony projection about halfway down the outer margin of the foot.

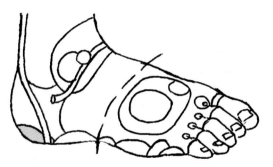

# 31 Ovaries and Testes

The two ovaries in females are the reproductive glands which produce the female hormones, oestrogen and progesterone, and the ova, or female sex cells. From puberty to menopause, the menstrual cycle takes place. This causes hormones to be produced in differing amounts to help the development and release of an egg each month and to act on other parts of the reproductive system, including the uterus, to prepare it to receive a fertilised ovum.

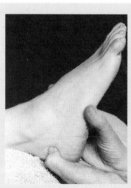

## TREATMENT

*Work with the left thumb (or finger pressure) on the point halfway between the tip of the outer ankle bone and the very back of the heel.*

The testes (testicles) in males are the male reproductive glands and are suspended outside the body in the scrotum. The testes produce the sperm, the mobile sex cells, and the male hormone, testosterone, which at puberty develops the male sexual characteristics and maintains these throughout life, though testosterone levels do decrease as men get older.

## REFLEXOLOGY AREA

The reflex areas for the ovaries/testes are found in both feet halfway between the outer ankle bone and the back of the heel.

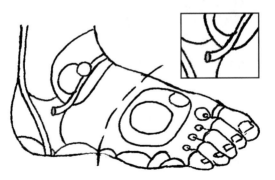

# 32 Fallopian Tubes and Vas Deferens

The Fallopian tubes in females extend from the ovaries on each side of the pelvis to the uterus in the centre of the pelvis. The ova, released at ovulation from the ovaries, travel down the Fallopian tubes to the uterus. Fertilisation of an ovum usually takes place in the Fallopian tube.

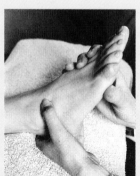

## TREATMENT

*Work over the top of the foot, in front of the ankle bones, from the ovary/testis reflex on the outer side to the uterus/prostate point on the inner side using the left thumb (or finger pressure).*

The vas deferens in males is one of the two tubules along which the sperm travel from the testes to the penis.

## REFLEXOLOGY AREA

The reflex areas for the Fallopian tubes/vas deferens are found across the top of both feet in front of the ankles between the reflex areas for the ovaries/testes and uterus/prostate.

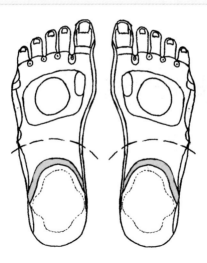

# 33 Uterus and Prostate Gland

The uterus (womb) in females is situated centrally in the pelvic region behind the bladder. It is a muscular pear-shaped organ. From the time of puberty to the menopause it goes through a cycle of changes in response to the female hormones to prepare it to receive a fertilised ovum and thus for pregnancy. If fertilisation does not occur then the lining

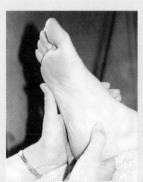

## TREATMENT

*Work with the left or right thumb (or finger pressure) on the point half way between the tip of the inner ankle bone and the very back of the heel.*

of the uterus is shed together with blood (menstruation) at the end of each menstrual cycle.

The prostate gland in males is situated just below the bladder and produces a lubricating fluid which helps the transport of the sperm.

## REFLEXOLOGY AREA

The reflex areas for the uterus/prostate gland are found in both feet halfway between the inner ankle bone and the back of the heel, and there is also an additional reflex area located up the back of the leg for a few inches on either side of the Achilles tendon.

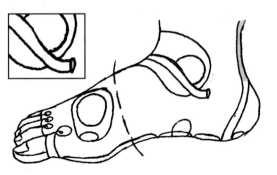

# **34** Lymphatic System

The lymphatic system is situated throughout the body and is rather like a secondary circulatory system to the blood. Lymph vessels absorb and cleanse a fluid called lymph before discharging it back into the bloodstream. The function of the lymph vessels is to drain the excess tissue

## TREATMENT

**(34a)** *Work the top of the foot from the roots of the toes down to above the ankle bones. Finger pressure may be used. Start on the inner side of the foot at the root of the big toe and second toe.*

## REFLEXOLOGY AREA

The reflex areas for the lymphatic system are found in both feet, occupying an area on the top of the foot. At the bases of the webs of the toes are found the reflexes to the upper lymph nodes (those of the head and neck), then down the foot over the metatarsal bones is the area for the thoracic lymph and upper abdominal lymph.

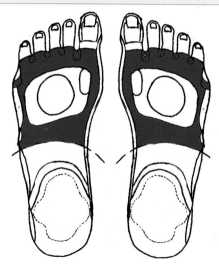

fluid. Before lymph is returned to the bloodstream the
excess fluid must first pass through areas known as 'lymph
nodes'. These nodes are where cells act to purify the lymph
by removing any foreign or damaging substances that might
be present. Lymph nodes are situated at various sites in the
body in the head, neck, armpit, elbow, chest, abdomen,
pelvis, groin and knee.

**(34b)** *Having done all the areas on the top of the foot you
will have overlapped the breast reflex just above diaphragm
level in zones 2, 3, and 4. Work the reflexes for the
lymphatics of the pelvis and the groin by using finger
pressure above and around the ankle bones on both sides of
the feet.*

## REFLEXOLOGY AREA

Below waist level is the area relating to the abdominal lymph, leading to the area over and around the ankles which relates to the reflex areas for the lymph nodes of the pelvis and groin.

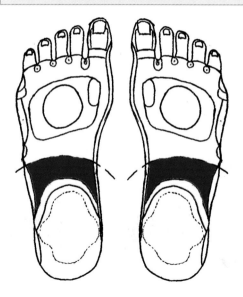

# 35 Lymphatic Drainage

After the lymph has passed through the body's lymph nodes and been cleansed by the lymph vessels, the vessels drain the excess tissue fluid back into the bloodstream.

## TREATMENT

*Pinch the area just below the web between the big toe and the second toe with the second finger on the top of the foot and the thumb on the sole of the foot.*

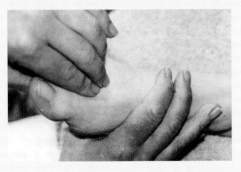

## REFLEXOLOGY AREA

The reflex areas for the lymph drainage point are found in both feet between the big toe and the second toe.

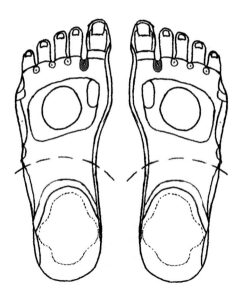

# Exercises

### E1. ROTATION OF TOES

Use the right hand to support the base of the right big toe joint from the inner foot and use the left hand to hold the toe near to the base and rotate the toe. Keeping the hands in the same position, rotate all of the other toes. You may need to change the hands round to rotate the fourth and fifth toes.

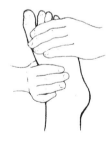

### E2. 'WRINGING' OF FOOT

Place the left hand round the little toe side of the foot with the fingers on the top of the foot and the thumb underneath, place the right hand similarly round the inner side of the foot, wring the hands apart so as to spread apart the bones of the feet.

## E3. 'KNEADING' OF FOOT

Using the flat surface of a clenched fist, press up at diaphragm level on the sole of the foot, put the other hand flat on the top of the foot and press the hands against each other, rotating at the same time.

## E4. ROTATION OF ANKLE

Place the left hand under the heel to raise the foot very slightly, use the right hand to support the toes, rotate the ankle round a few times in one direction and then in the other direction.

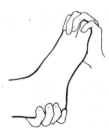

# LEFT FOOT

Follow the same order as for the right foot, but include within the order: the heart, the spleen, the large intestine.

## 15b Heart

The heart is found in the chest nearly centrally, just above the diaphragm, with one third to the right side and two thirds to the left. The size of a clenched fist, it is divided into four chambers with an upper and a lower chamber (the

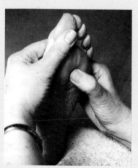

### TREATMENT

*With the right thumb work the area in zones 3 and 2 just above diaphragm level.*

'atrium' and 'ventricle') on each side. The heart pumps blood round the body. Oxygenated blood leaves the left side of the heart to enter the arteries via the aorta; deoxygenated blood returns to the right side via the veins.

## REFLEXOLOGY AREA

The reflex area for the heart is found in the left foot over the ball of the foot in longitudinal zones 2 and 3 just above diaphragm level.

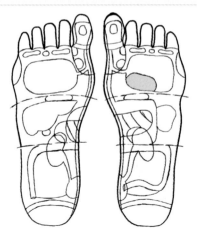

# 17b Spleen

The spleen is found above the waist on the left side of the body. It is important for breaking down old red blood cells and for activating new white blood cells which will play an important part in the body's defence system.

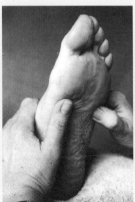

## TREATMENT

*Using the right thumb, work from zone 5 to zone 4, filling in the area between diaphragm and waist level.*

## REFLEXOLOGY AREA

The reflex area for the spleen is found in the left foot in longitudinal zones 4 and 5 between diaphragm and waist level.

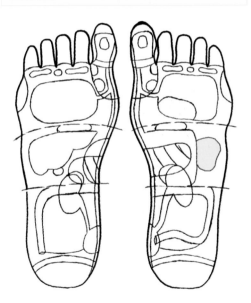

# 21a Large Intestine

(transverse colon, descending colon,
sigmoid colon, rectum)

On the left side of the body the large intestine heads
downwards as the descending colon before bending back
towards the centre as the sigmoid colon. The sigmoid colon
leads into the rectum, which leads into the anus.

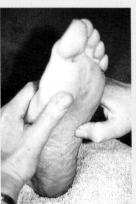

## TREATMENT

**(21a)** *Transverse
colon: Use the left
thumb to work across
at waist level from
zone 1 to zone 4/5.*

*Descending colon: Use
the right thumb to
work down from waist
level in zones 4/5 to
just above the pad of
the heel.*

## REFLEXOLOGY AREA

The reflex areas for the large intestine start with the ileo-caecal valve (right foot, longitudinal zones 4 and 5) and finish with the ascending colon at waist level. The transverse colon starts in zones 4 and 5 at waist level and travels over to the left foot (zones 4 and 5).

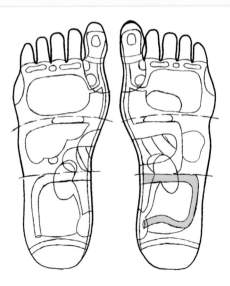

The main function of the large intestine is to eliminate the undigested food that reaches it from the small intestine in the form of faeces. As the food travels through the large intestine water is reabsorbed back into the body.

**(21b)** *Sigmoid colon and rectum: Use the right thumb to work from zone 4/5 just above the pad of the heel across the sole of the foot to zone 1 (rectum).*

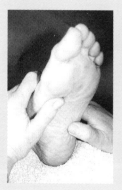
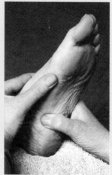

## REFLEXOLOGY AREA

The reflex area for the descending colon travels from waist level (in longitudinal zones 4 and 5) to just above the pad of the heel on the left foot. The sigmoid colon travels back to the centre across all zones finishing in zone 1 with the rectum/anus reflex area.

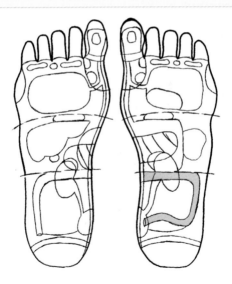

# Exercise

## E5 SOLAR PLEXUS BREATHING (BOTH FEET TOGETHER AT VERY END OF TREATMENT)

Place the right thumb on the solar plexus reflex on the right foot and the left thumb on the solar plexus reflex on the left foot. Apply pressure to the reflex as the patient takes a deep breath in, and at the same time ease the feet upwards slightly, towards the patient. Then as they breathe out ease the pressure off the solar plexus reflex and ease the feet down. Repeat three or four times.

For self treatment it will not be appropriate to do the solar plexus breathing with both feet together, so this exercise would be done to each foot individually.

## NOTE

General body parts that have not been referred to will still have been treated, since the whole of each foot treats the whole of the body. There are overlaps between certain parts of the body, and the same applies to the reflex areas. This means that in some areas more than one body part will be represented. When treating a particular reflex area, every aspect of the corresponding area of the body is treated, so not only are the actual organs or glands there focused on, but also the blood supply, the nerves, the muscles of the area and the skin covering the area. Thus to treat the skin of a particular part, for example the face, the face reflex would need to be worked.

## ZONE-RELATED AREAS

The zone-related areas described by Dr Fitzgerald can also be used with reflexology. There is a special relationship between the arm and the leg on the same side of the body because they are in the same longitudinal zones, and also between the shoulder and the hip, the elbow and the knee, the hand and the foot, the fingers and the toes. Thus, in addition to reflexology of the feet, zone-related areas can be worked on directly for specific problems. Try rubbing the right elbow when there is a pain in the right knee or massaging the left elbow when there's pain in the left knee.

# SPECIFIC TREATMENTS

Some common ailments that affect the body will now be
considered, with a brief description of the condition and
possible symptoms associated with it. The most important
reflex areas for treating the condition will be mentioned,
but treatment should always be given to all the reflex areas
in both feet, in order to treat the body as a whole. The
important reflex areas mentioned are those that require
extra attention, as they may be helpful in treating both
symptoms present in the condition and possible causes of it.
Not all the reflex areas mentioned may be important in a
particular case. The numbers in brackets after each reflex
area relate to that area's position within the Recommended
Order of Treatment (*see pages 56–57*).

## ACNE

Acne is often associated with puberty and results in cysts
forming on the skin, particularly on the face, chest and the
upper back. These sometimes scar. There is an increased
secretion of sebum by the sebaceous glands, which blocks
the sebaceous ducts and hair follicles in the skin. As well
as the effect of hormone levels, dietary factors may be
a cause.

Important reflex areas: face (6), adrenals (25), ovaries or testes (31), pituitary (1), solar plexus (16), lymphatics (34), liver and gall bladder (17)

## AIDS

The condition of AIDS results from the presence of the human immuno-deficiency virus (HIV) in the body. This attacks a weakened immune system and gives rise to AIDS, which may start with flu-like symptoms but progresses with the development of infections such as pneumonia – which involves the lungs – diarrhoea and weight loss, due to infection in the digestive tract. There are also skin eruptions.

Important reflex areas: lymphatics (34), spleen (17b), lungs (15), large intestine (21), adrenals (25)

## ALLERGIES

More and more people are suffering from allergies. When allergies develop there is an oversensitivity of a part of the body to certain substances. Allergic reactions include digestive problems, eczema, asthma and migraines. Reflexology treatment will help to reduce the body's oversensitivity and thus the allergic response.

Important reflex areas: adrenals (25), spleen (17b), lymphatics (34), stomach (18), large intestine (21), lungs (15), top of head (4)

## ANGINA

With angina, a person will experience short sharp pains in the chest region where the heart is situated, usually following some exertion. This occurs due to a decreased blood supply and therefore a lack of oxygen to the heart muscle.

Important reflex areas: heart (15b), solar plexus (16), adrenals (25), lungs (15)

## ARTHRITIS

Arthritis involves pain and inflammation of a joint. There are many different forms, which include osteoarthritis, rheumatoid arthritis and gout, but from the reflexology angle the approach to treatment will be similar. The joints most commonly affected are the hips, knees, spine and fingers. With gout it is often the big toe joint that is affected. The eliminating organs are also important – i.e. the kidneys, intestines and liver – to help clear toxins from the body.

Important reflex areas: adrenals (25), hips (30), knees (29), spine (5), kidneys (24), large intestine (21), liver (17)

## ASTHMA

The asthmatic will experience bouts of breathlessness, tightness in the chest and throat and wheezy breathing. During an asthmatic attack the muscles of the bronchi go into spasm and constrict the airways, and there is also increased mucus production which blocks the airways further. Asthma may be due to an allergy, such as to dust, pollen, feathers or animals, or may occur in later life in those with a history of respiratory problems. Stress can also be the cause of an asthma attack.

> Important reflex areas: lungs (15), adrenals (25), heart (15b), solar plexus (16), sinuses (7)

## BACK PROBLEMS – STIFF NECK, LUMBAGO

Back problems may involve such things as pulled muscles, strained ligaments or slipped discs, and although it is not possible to diagnose the exact problem with reflexology, it is possible to treat these conditions. However, should a medical diagnosis not have been made, and if a person has had two or three reflexology treatments without improvement, then it is important to refer the patient to a person who can make a thorough diagnosis. Back problems are so common that often when working the reflex area to the spine it will appear tender, and on questioning the patient it will be found that from time to time they suffer from pain in the back. Treatment can help to strengthen and relieve this area. The most common regions affected are the cervical region (neck problems) and the lumbar region (lower backache, lumbago). Another consideration with a back problem is that the nerves from the affected region may be involved and thus the nerve supply to different areas of the body affected, impairing the correct functioning of these areas. Neck problems lead to shoulder and arm problems; lower back problems may lead to problems in the leg, such as sciatica.

> Important reflex areas: spine (5), neck (2), shoulders (12), arms (13), legs (29, 30), sacro-iliac joints (27), sciatic nerves (26)

## BRONCHITIS

Bronchitis is inflammation of the bronchi – the tubes that lead from the windpipe to the lungs. This may be associated with infection such as with a cold or 'flu, or a chronic condition may result from persistent exposure to irritants such as cigarette smoke, car fumes and other atmospheric pollutants.

> Important reflex areas: lungs (15), lymphatics (34), adrenals (25), sinuses (7)

## CANCER

Cancer cells will develop in the body when its defence system is unable to destroy them, and these can settle in many different areas such as the lungs, cervix, breast, stomach and large intestine (colon). Reflexology can be used with other natural therapies and orthodox treatments to help strengthen the body's immune system. Where orthodox treatment is being received, treatment may help the body cope with the side-effects experienced. Treatment can also be given to those seriously ill with cancer to help with relaxation, pain relief and general well-being.

Important reflex areas: lymphatics (34), spleen (17b), lungs (15), uterus (33), breasts (34), stomach (18), large intestine (21), solar plexus (16)

## CARPAL TUNNEL SYNDROME

This is a wrist problem where the nerves entering the wrist through a fibrous band at the joint called the carpal tunnel become compressed, causing pain and numbness in part of the hand.

Important reflex areas: arms and elbows (13), neck (2), spine – cervical (5), adrenals (25)

## CATARACTS

When a cataract develops, the lens of the eye loses its opacity. The process starts at the edge of the lens and spreads towards the centre, reducing vision. This is a fairly common complaint in the elderly and for those with diabetes.

Important reflex areas: eyes (9), kidneys (24), pancreas (19)

# CHILBLAINS

Poor circulation can lead to chilblains, where red, oval swellings appear on the fingers or toes which are intensely itchy. These will appear when the areas get cold, especially if it is also damp. Problems with the nerve supply from the spine may be involved, including the upper spine if the fingers are affected and the lower spine if the toes are affected. Poor elimination through the digestive tract may be causing congestion in the body and so affecting circulation.

Important reflex areas: heart (15b), adrenals (25), spine (5), small intestine (20), large intestine (21), liver (17)

# COLITIS

Colitis is inflammation of the colon (large intestine); one form of it is irritable bowel syndrome (IBS). Another more serious form is ulcerative colitis, where ulcers develop in the walls of the large intestine. Symptoms include abdominal pain and diarrhoea with blood in the stools due to bleeding from the ulcers. In severe cases anaemia and dehydration can result.

Important reflex areas: large intestine (21), small intestine (20), adrenals (25)

## CONJUNCTIVITIS

This is a common infection where the eye becomes red and itchy. It can also be caused by an allergic reaction. Rubbing the affected eye and then the other eye may easily cause the infection to spread to both eyes. Those with a tendency towards eye infections such as conjunctivitis can work the reflex areas to try to prevent these frequent nuisances.

Important reflex areas: eyes (9), upper lymphatics (34), adrenals (25)

## CONSTIPATION

Constipation involves irregular bowel movements and difficulty with emptying the bowel. It may be linked to lack of roughage in the diet, lack of fluid intake, poor muscle tone in the intestines or poor nerve supply to the area. Since the large intestine is an important eliminating organ, if it is not working then toxins are accumulating in the body and can lead to other conditions such as headaches, skin problems, sinus problems and circulatory problems.

Important reflex areas: large intestine (21), small intestine (20), adrenals (25), solar plexus (16), spine (5), top of head and brain (4), sinuses (7)

# CYSTITIS

Cystitis is inflammation and infection of the bladder. It will cause an increased need to empty the bladder and often a burning sensation on passing urine. Those who suffer from cystitis may find the condition recurs when they get tired and run down. Regular reflexology treatment may help to strengthen this area and the lymph system so that repeated infections do not occur.

Important reflex areas: bladder (22), ureter tubes (23), kidneys (24), adrenals (25), pelvic lymphatics (34)

# DEAFNESS

Deafness may be due to a number of factors, and with age the hearing often deteriorates. A simple cause may be wax in the ear which is blocking the pathway down to the ear drum and thus affecting normal hearing. Other problems can include damage to the ear drum or to the middle ear, including blocked eustachian tubes which may be caused by a cold. Deafness can also stem from damage to the hearing receptors in the inner ear or to the hearing areas of the brain.

Important reflex areas: ears (11), Eustachian tubes (10), side of head and brain (3), neck (2), spine – cervical (5), solar plexus (16), adrenals (25)

## DERMATITIS

With dermatitis there is inflammation of the skin due to allergy and the condition is very similar to eczema. An itchy rash develops and often the face, eyes, arms and elbows can be affected.

Important reflex areas: face (6), eyes (9), arms and elbows (13), adrenals (25), solar plexus (16), lymphatics (34)

## DIABETES

In the condition of diabetes there is a deficiency of the hormone insulin, usually caused by the pancreas not producing sufficient insulin. As the disorder progresses, other parts of the body can be affected and especially the eyes, the kidneys, the blood circulation and the lymphatic system. Particular care must be taken if a diabetic is taking insulin, since reflexology treatment may encourage the pancreas to start to produce more insulin, requiring the medication taken to be adjusted.

Important reflex areas: pancreas (19), liver (17), adrenals (25), eyes (9), kidneys (24), heart (15b), lymphatics (34)

## DIARRHOEA

The term diarrhoea refers to increased frequency in emptying the bowel with a greater fluid content to the stools. Short term, it is the body's way of removing anything unsuitable and is not a problem, but long term there is a risk of dehydration, since undigested food has not spent long enough in the large intestine for water to be reabsorbed. Also the food will have passed through the small intestine too quickly to allow the correct breakdown and absorption.

Important reflex areas: large intestine (21), small intestine (20), adrenals (25), lymphatics (34)

## DRY EYES

When the eyes are dry, insufficient tears are being produced. It is the tears that help to lubricate the eyes and remove dirt and dust, which are irritants, so when the eyes dry they also get sore and itchy.

Important reflex areas: eyes (9), upper lymphatics (34), adrenals (25)

## EARACHE AND EAR INFECTIONS

Earache and ear infections are common, and pain felt in the ear will usually be due to infection, particularly in the middle ear. Any infection must be treated quickly so that it does not spread to the inner ear and affect hearing/balance. Those with a tendency towards ear infections can work reflexes to try to prevent them.

Important reflex areas: ears (11), Eustachian tubes (10), lymphatics – upper (34), side of head and brain (3), solar plexus (16), adrenals (25)

## ECZEMA

With eczema the skin is dry, flaky and itchy. It can often occur in babies and young children, where it results from an allergy, especially to cow's milk. Many youngsters grow out of the condition but it can recur in adult life, when it is often linked with allergy, dietary factors and stress. The common sites for eczema are the face, ears, arms and legs – particularly in the creases of the joints.

Important reflex areas : face (6), ears (11), arms (13), legs (29, 30), adrenals (25), solar plexus (16), lymphatics (34)

## FOOT PROBLEMS

Sometimes people misunderstand what reflexology treatment involves and expect that since it is applied to the feet then the treatment is for foot problems. This is not so: reflexology is treating problems in the body *through* the feet. Problems involving the feet themseves such as bunions, corns or ingrowing toe-nails, are best dealt with by the podiatrist. However, in some instances reflexology treatment may be beneficial and the effect of the general massage to all areas of the feet may help in easing foot pain, though it might aggravate the condition if arthritis, gout or severe osteoporosis is present. It will often improve poor circulation in the feet and also problems with swollen feet and ankles.

## GALLSTONES

Gallstones are supposedly more common in females who are 'fair, fat, fertile and flatulent'! These small stones that form in the gall bladder are usually made up of cholesterol and are often associated with a diet high in fats. If the stones are small then it may be possible to help them to be passed and they will move down in the bile from the gall bladder to the small intestine and then be eliminated through the large intestine.

Important reflex areas: liver and gall bladder (17), small intestine (20)

## GLAUCOMA

Glaucoma is a more serious eye problem where there is an increase in pressure within the eyeball. Symptoms may include painful eyes, reduced vision, seeing coloured haloes around lights, and headaches. It occurs most commonly in the elderly.

Important reflex areas: eyes (9), neck (2), top of head and brain (4), kidneys (24)

# HEADACHES AND MIGRAINES

Headaches are common conditions which most people suffer from at some time. A migraine is a severe headache, sometimes accompanied by visual disturbances and feelings of nausea.

There are many possible causes of headaches and migraines. These include:

- allergy to certain foods or other substances
- dietary factors such as too much fat in the diet
- the menstrual cycle or the menopause in women
- neck and upper spine problems
- sinus congestion
- eye strain
- constipation, leading to a build-up of toxins in the system
- high blood pressure
- tension
- stress

Often the patient will be aware of the cause, but if not it is usually possible to find it by establishing which reflex areas are tender. Migraine sufferers can be helped by reflexology either clearing the condition or reducing the frequency and severity of attacks.

Important reflex areas: top of the head (4), side of the head (3), neck (2), spine – cervical (5), solar plexus (16), liver and gall bladder (17), ovaries (31), sinuses (7), eyes (9), large intestine (21), heart (15b), kidneys (24), adrenals (25)

## HIGH BLOOD PRESSURE

One of the common causes of high blood pressure is stress, though other factors may include obesity, heart or kidney disease and dietary factors such as excess alcohol and smoking. Symptoms that may be experienced include headaches, dizziness, ringing in the ears, breathlessness, chest pain and coughing. Eyesight too may be affected. In some cases, a person may have high blood pressure without being aware of any symptoms. Where high blood pressure is present there is added strain on the heart, the blood vessels and the kidneys.

Important reflex areas: heart (15b), adrenals (25), kidneys (24), pituitary (1), top of head (4), ears (11), eyes (9), solar plexus (16)

## IMPAIRED VISION

Many people suffer from eyesight problems, and although reflexology may not reverse this problem it may help to prevent deterioration of the eyesight. By working the eye reflex, the eye's muscles will be stimulated to function more efficiently if they have become lazy and the eye's nerves will also be treated.

> Important reflex areas: eyes (9), neck (2), spine – cervical (5), kidneys (24), adrenals (25)

## INCONTINENCE

Incontinence means inability to control the emptying of the bladder and may be due to damage to the nerve supply to the bladder or involve weakness in the pelvic muscles. In children, bed-wetting may occur due to emotional factors, but the problem can still be helped with reflexology.

> Important reflex areas: bladder (22), ureter tubes (23), kidneys (24), adrenals (25), lymphatics – pelvic (34), spine – lumbar and sacral (5)

## INDIGESTION

Indigestion is pain in the stomach region and is due not only to the types of foods eaten but to the way they are eaten. Often indigestion is linked to eating too quickly or in a stressed state.

> Important reflex areas: stomach (18), solar plexus (16), adrenals (25)

# INFECTIONS

Infections of different parts of the body will occur when the body's own defence system is not strong enough to resist the infection. General conditions such as influenza may result, or more specific problems such as ear or bladder infections. The reflexology treatment may help to clear an infection, but more importantly it may also help to strengthen the body's defence system so as to prevent infections occurring in the future.

> Important reflex areas: lymphatics (34), spleen (17b),
> sinuses (7), ears (11), bladder (22)

# INFERTILITY

Infertility is the inability to conceive and may be related to stress, hormone levels, a failure to ovulate, a low sperm count or a blocked fallopian tube.

> Important reflex areas: ovaries (31), uterus (33), Fallopian
> tubes (32), pituitary (1), thyroid and parathyroids (14),
> adrenals (25), solar plexus (16)

# INSOMNIA AND SLEEP PROBLEMS

Many people suffer from these problems, which may involve having difficulty in getting to sleep or waking during the night and not being able to return to sleep. They can be due

to stress and worry, depression or pain – such as arthritic
pain or severe earache – or may result from time differences,
as with jet-lag.

Important reflex areas: pituitary (1), head and brain (3,4),
solar plexus (16), adrenals (25), spine (5), hips (30),
knees (29), ears (11)

## IRRITABLE BOWEL SYNDROME (IBS)

Irritable bowel syndrome is relatively self-explanatory.
Symptoms include:

• pains in the abdomen

• constipation and diarrhoea

• an excess of mucus in the stools

There may also be flatulence, distension in the abdomen and
abdominal rumblings. The condition is thought to be stress-
related, though certain foods can also affect it.

Important reflex areas: large intestine (21), small
intestine (20), adrenals (25), solar plexus (16)

## KIDNEY STONES

Stones can form in the kidney and are often only about the
size of a grape pip, though they can be larger. They are
usually made up of calcium, and provided they are small

may be passed from the kidney in the urine. As the stone passes down the ureter tube to the bladder, pain may be felt.

Important reflex areas: kidneys (24), ureter tubes (23), bladder (22), adrenals (25), thyroid and parathyroids (14)

## KNEE PROBLEMS

Knee problems may involve the ligaments of the knee or its cartilages. Problems can develop from overuse, and the knee is a common site of injury in sports players.

Important reflex areas: knees (29), hips (30), spine – lower (5), adrenals (25)

## MASTITIS

In mastitis there is inflammation of the breasts with oedema, and this can occur before a period. The breast may also feel lumpy, and there could be a discharge from the nipple. It can also occur in those who are breastfeeding.

Important reflex areas: lymphatics and breast (34), adrenals (25)

## ME

With the condition of myalgic encephalomyelitis (ME), chronic fatigue syndrome, the person develops extreme fatigue and muscle weakness following an infection, and this can last for months or years after the infection has cleared. There may also be disturbances of the digestive system. Sometimes when a course is commenced a person with ME can feel more tired after treatment but this effect will soon pass.

Important reflex areas: lymphatics (34), spleen (17b), adrenals (25), stomach (18), small intestine (20), large intestine (21)

## MENOPAUSAL PROBLEMS

Many women experience problems at the time of the menopause, as the body has to adjust to the reduced levels of the female sex hormones. These problems can include such symptoms as hot flushes, depression, fatigue, migraines, digestive and urinary problems and osteoporosis. Reflexology treatment will not prevent the menopause but will help the body adjust to the changes taking place. Often women follow a course of treatment as they approach the menopause to try to prevent strong symptoms developing.

Important reflex areas: ovaries (31), uterus (33), pituitary (1), thyroid and parathyroids (14), adrenals (25), top of head (4), large intestine (21), bladder (22)

## MOUTH ULCERS

Mouth ulcers are sores on the gums which may result from poor mouth hygiene or from foods that are eaten that irritate the gums.

> Important reflex areas: teeth (8), face (6), lymphatics –
> upper (34), adrenals (25)

## MS

With Multiple Sclerosis, the transmission of the nerve impulses is impaired and symptoms such as muscle weakness, reduced control of movements, loss of balance and loss of sensation may develop. Sometimes the eyes can be affected. There can be periods of remission when the symptoms disappear but they then return as the condition progresses.

With the more serious disorders of the nervous system such as stroke, Parkinson's disease and MS, symptoms such as constipation or a loss of control over emptying the bladder can respond well to treatment. More obvious improvements can take time, though people often express a sense of feeling better in themselves and coping better with daily tasks. It may well be that treatment is needed over a considerable period of time, maybe months or years, to try to achieve improvement or to halt the deterioration of the condition.

Important reflex areas: head and brain (1, 3, 4), neck (2), spine (5), arms (13), legs (29, 30), eyes (9), bladder (22), large intestine (21), adrenals (25)

## PALPITATIONS

Palpitations occur when the heart is beating so much more forcefully and faster than usual that the person becomes aware of their heart beating. They may be associated with anxiety or stress or with an overactive thyroid gland.

Important reflex areas: heart (15b), solar plexus (16), adrenals (25), thyroid (14)

## PARKINSON'S DISEASE

With Parkinson's disease, there is damage to the nervous system controlling the muscles. This can lead to stiffness/weakness in the muscles, with movement becoming uncoordinated. There may be a tremor – noticeable in the hands and legs – and a 'mask-like' look can develop due to the face muscles not functioning correctly.

Important reflex areas: head and brain (1, 3, 4), neck (2), spine (5), adrenals (25), arms (13), legs (29, 30), face (6), bladder (22), large intestine (21)

# PERIODS – ABSENCE OF

The first consideration here must be pregnancy or menopause. It may otherwise be due to hormone imbalance, ovarian problems, disorders of the thyroid or adrenal glands. It is often seen when there has been weight loss or after stopping the contraceptive pill.

Important reflex areas: ovaries (31), Fallopian tubes (32), uterus (33), pituitary (1), thyroid (14), adrenals (25)

# PERIODS – PAINFUL

The pain associated with menstruation may occur for a few days before a period starts or for the first few days of the period. As well as pain, there may be a feeling of bloating of the abdomen together with headaches or migraines, joint and back pains and nausea. It will usually relate to a problem with the uterus.

Important reflex areas: ovaries (31), Fallopian tubes (32), uterus (33), pituitary (1), thyroid (14), adrenals (25), lymphatics – abdominal (34), top of head (4), spine (5), knees (29), stomach (18)

# PMS

Over one hundred and fifty different symptoms can be attributable to Pre-Menstrual Syndrome (or PMS) and these can occur for as long as ten days before a period. Symptoms can include mood changes – anxiety, irritability, lack of concentration – migraines, backache, breast discomfort, abdominal distension, fluid retention and constipation.

Important reflex areas: ovaries (31), Fallopian tubes (32), uterus (33), pituitary (1), thyroid (14), adrenals (25), head and brain (3, 4), spine (5), lymphatics (34), kidneys (24), large intestine (21)

## PROSTATE GLAND – ENLARGED

This problem commonly affects men as they get older and as the prostate gland enlarges, pressing up on the bladder and giving the impression of a greater sense of fullness there and therefore an increased need to empty it. This condition can be particularly troublesome at night, causing men to have interrupted sleep. Reflexology may help to alleviate the problem and may reduce the need to empty the bladder so frequently.

Important reflex areas: prostate (33), bladder (22), ureter tubes (23), kidneys (24), adrenals (25), lymphatics – pelvic (34)

## PSORIASIS

With psoriasis, slightly raised red patches appear on the skin, covered by silver scales which flake off leaving a red map-like rash. Common areas to be affected are the elbows, knees and scalp. Linked to the psoriasis, the nails are often pitted and ridged and arthritis can develop in the joints.

Important reflex areas: top of head (4), arms (13), knees (29), adrenals (25), solar plexus (16), lymphatics (34)

## RHINITIS AND HAY FEVER

With rhinitis there is inflammation of the membranes of the nose due to an allergy to substances such as dust, animal hairs and flowers. With hay fever the allergy is to grass pollens. Symptoms include a streaming (or sometimes blocked) nose, sneezing and watering of the eyes.

These reactions are due to an oversensitivity of the mucous membranes, and treatment can help reduce this condition. Where the allergy is a seasonal one, such as with hay fever, it is best to treat the person before the time of year when they are affected, to try in the first instance to prevent the attack and in the second to reduce its impact.

Important reflex areas : sinuses (7), face (6), eyes (9), adrenals (25), lymphatics – upper (34)

## RSI

A repetitive strain injury is one caused by repetitive use of an area, but the term RSI is often used to refer to problems involving the wrist joint. A common cause of this injury is using a computer keyboard or typewriter.

> Important reflex areas: arms and elbows (13), neck (2), spine – cervical (5), adrenals (25)

## SCIATICA

The sciatic nerve which runs from the lower back down the back of the leg can become inflamed and the condition of sciatica results, causing pain along any part of the region which the nerve supplies. Sciatica will usually result from a problem with the lower spine or the pelvis.

> Important reflex areas: sciatic nerves (26), spine – lumbar, sacral (5), sacro-iliac joint (27), muscles of the pelvis (28), hips (30), knees (29), adrenals (25)

## SHOULDER PROBLEMS

Problems with the shoulder often result from trouble in the neck or upper spine. Common shoulder problems in women result from carrying bags on their shoulder or carrying children. Another common condition is a frozen shoulder, where the joint becomes very painful and has restricted movement. Treatment may be helpful whether the problem is associated with the muscles or the ligaments of the shoulder joint.

> Important reflex areas: shoulders (12), neck (2), spine –
> cervical, thoracic (5), arms and elbows (13)

## SINUSITIS AND CATARRH

Many people suffer from congestion in the nose and sinuses,
probably due to such factors as air pollution, working in air-
conditioned offices, double-glazing in houses where
windows are rarely opened or a general lack of fresh air.
With sinusitis there may also be pain in the face and around
the eyes, where the sinuses are positioned. Following
treatment it is quite common for the nose and the sinuses to
clear and for cold-like symptoms to develop as the excess
mucus is cleared. This reaction occurs very readily and it
is important not to overwork the sinus areas when first
treating a patient.

> Important reflex areas: sinuses (7), face (6), Eustachian
> tubes (10), eyes (9), adrenals (25), ileo-caecal valve (21)

## SORE THROATS – TONSILLITIS, LARYNGITIS

A sore throat is due to infection and may develop on its own
or accompany a cold. The tonsils are found in the throat in
the region called the pharynx and are made up of lymph
tissue. They enlarge when infection occurs, and if there are
repeated infections they can remain enlarged and become
ulcerated. The condition 'tonsillitis' is an inflammation of

the tonsils more common in children, when the tonsils are more active. Laryngitis involves inflammation of the larynx or voice box, and when this occurs the voice will be affected and may even be lost temporarily.

> Important reflex areas: face (6), lymphatics – upper (34), sinuses (7), adrenals (25)

## STRESS

Stress is probably the most common condition experienced in modern times and can result in a range of different conditions such as migraines, insomnia, eczema, asthma and irritable bowel syndrome – all of which have been discussed above. The general relaxing effect of reflexology treatment can be very beneficial to people suffering from stress, as can the one-to-one contact with the practitioner for a whole hour when problems can be discussed. Although treatment may not be able to remove external stress factors such as family or work situations, often people find that they are able to cope with the stress better as a result of treatment.

> Important reflex areas: adrenals (25), solar plexus (16)

## STROKE

With a stroke or cerebral haemorrhage a blood clot develops in the cerebral region of the brain. The clot will usually be on one side of the brain, and the result of a stroke will be a partial or total paralysis on the opposite side of the body to the side of the brain affected, since the right side of the brain controls the muscles of the left side of the body and the left side of the brain controls the right side of the body. Speech may also be affected. Factors such as high blood pressure and poor circulation may lead to a stroke. Depending on the severity of the stroke, some patients will make a better recovery than others. In general, the sooner a patient is treated after suffering a stroke, the better the results.

> Important reflex areas: head and brain (1, 3, 4), neck (2), spine (5), heart (15b), adrenals (25), arms (13), legs (29, 30), face (6)

## TENNIS ELBOW

With tennis elbow there is inflammation of the outer side of the elbow. It need not occur from playing tennis and can be caused by a variety of activities including gardening and other tasks involving repeated rotation of the forearm.

> Important reflex areas: arms and elbows (13), neck (2), spine – cervical (5), adrenals (25)

## THYROID IMBALANCE

The thyroid gland can quite commonly be found to be imbalanced, becoming overactive or underactive. With an overactive thyroid, the metabolism speeds up and the person becomes nervy and anxious, with an increased heart rate, sweating, weight loss even though the appetite is good, diarrhoea and protruding eyes. With an underactive thyroid, the metabolism slows down, so the person becomes slow and sluggish, feels cold, gains weight and becomes puffy in the face.

Important reflex areas: thyroid (14), pituitary (1), heart (15b), large intestine (21), eyes (9), face (6)

## TINNITUS

With tinnitus a person experiences noises in the ear. The noise may be a persistent ringing, buzzing or humming, and often becomes more noticeable when it is quiet, which makes it especially difficult for a person with tinnitus to relax or go off to sleep.

Important reflex areas : ears (11), Eustachian tubes (10), side of head and brain (3), neck (2), spine – cervical (5), solar plexus (16), adrenals (25)

## TOOTHACHE

If there is persistent pain then a visit to the dentist is required, but reflexology may be able to help relieve toothache. The pain may be due to infection around the teeth or a cavity in the tooth.

Important reflex areas: teeth (8), face (6), lymphatics – upper (34), solar plexus (16)

# VARICOSE VEINS

Varicose veins commonly occur in the legs, where the veins become swollen and twisted. They may also be painful. They occur more as people get older but are more likely to be found in those who are overweight or who stand for long periods. Although it is unlikely that reflexology treatment will get rid of existing varicose veins, it can ease discomfort and improve circulation, which should help to prevent the formation of further varicose veins.

Important reflex areas: heart (15b), legs (29, 30), adrenals (25), spine (5), small intestine (20), large intestine (21) liver (17)

# VERTIGO

With vertigo, the balance mechanism of the inner ear is affected. People think that stationary objects around them are moving and may then feel dizzy, lose their balance and may fall.

Important reflex areas: ears (11), Eustachian tubes (10), side of head and brain (3), neck (2), spine – cervical (5), eyes (9), solar plexus (16), adrenals (25)

# Conclusion

So reflexology treatment can help a wide range of conditions. It may assist by clearing the problem up totally, or by lessening the extent of the symptoms, or by helping the person to cope better with their illness. Of course, not everyone will see the same degree of improvement.

Reflexology treatment is suitable for people of all ages – babies, young children, teenagers, adults and the elderly – and can be used to help minor or major symptoms. Not only does it help with ailments but it maintains overall health and encourages relaxation.

# POSSIBLE REACTIONS TO TREATMENT

Apart from the many benefits felt after a reflexology session, such as relaxation, calmness and well-being, there are a number of other common reactions that can occur which are natural and, before long, beneficial. These are sometimes called 'healing reactions' and mostly involve the body trying to rid itself of toxins which have built up in the various systems. The type of reactions that occur will largely depend on the systems of the body that are congested and therefore need to be rid of toxins. The following are possible common reactions:

## COLD-LIKE SYMPTOMS

The nose may start to stream as if a cold is starting, though sometimes a blocked nose may occur before the streaming. Sometimes a person may develop a cough, or cough more if they already have a cough and cough up mucus.

## INCREASED PASSING OF URINE

There may be an increase in the frequency of passing urine, and the urine might also have a different colour or odour from normal.

## INCREASED BOWEL ACTIVITY

There may not only be an increase in frequency of emptying the bowel but also an increase in the volume of the stools.

## AGGRAVATED SKIN CONDITIONS

A skin rash may worsen or a person may find they come out in spots, particularly on the face. There can sometimes be increased perspiration.

## HEADACHES

It is quite common with many natural therapies for people to experience a headache after treatment as toxins are stirred up in the body, ready to be cleared. Those who are already migraine sufferers may find that a migraine develops after treatment.

## THIRST

Sometimes people can feel very thirsty after treatment, and if this happens they should drink plenty of water.

## TEMPERATURE CHANGES

After treatment some people may go quite cold and shivery, and this can sometimes develop during the actual treatment session. This is a good sign and indicates that internal healing is taking place. The body temperature will usually return to normal within five or ten minutes after treatment has finished. Others may go quite hot during or after treatment, and look quite flushed in the face, and this indicates an increase in the blood circulation.

## ARTHRITIS

Those with arthritis may well find that the joints are more painful after treatment.

## PREVIOUS DISORDERS

Sometimes conditions which a person has had, particularly when these conditions have been suppressed by medication, may recur.

## DISRUPTED SLEEP PATTERNS

Most people find they sleep more deeply after treatment, though sometimes they may find their sleep is disturbed and that they are more aware of their dreams.

## EMOTIONAL REACTIONS

Although most people feel relaxed and calm after treatment, sometimes a person may feel depressed and weepy or show increased sensitivity and bad temper. Some people find they yawn a lot after treatment, which is a way of releasing emotions.

These reactions will normally occur within twenty-four to forty-eight hours of treatment and will most probably last for a similar length of time. They are only likely to occur after the first one or two treatments and will not always happen. Careful treatment will ensure that these reactions are not too severe, which could put a person off having further reflexology treatment and also cause additional stress by making them too ill to carry out their normal daily routine. It should also be noted that these reactions do not always happen, and that some people can recuperate from their conditions without showing any healing reactions.

# Useful Addresses

## UNITED KINGDOM

**The British Reflexology Association (BRA)**
Monks Orchard, Whitbourne, Worcester WR6 5RB
Tel: 01886-821207
Fax: 01886-822017
E-mail: bra@britreflex.co.uk

**The Bayly School of Reflexology is the official teaching body
of the British Reflexology Association** – address as above
E-mail: bayly@britreflex.co.uk

**Overseas representatives of the Bayly School of Reflexology:
Ms Julia Williams**
PO Box 564, Morayfield, Brisbane, Queensland 4506
Australia

**Mrs Kazuko Makino**
2-25-1-206 Sekido, Tama, Tokyo, Japan

**Mrs Cathy Wade**
PO Box 15020, Nairobi, Kenya

**Noelle Weyeneth**
80 avenue de France, Lausanne, Switzerland
Tel: 0041 216 469102

**The Foundation for Integrated Medicine (FIM)**
International House, 59 Compton Road, London N1 2YT
Tel: 020-7688-1881

Fax: 020-7688-1882
e-mail: enquiries@fimed.org

## EUROPE

**Reflexology in Europe Network**
Secretary, Bovenover 59, 1025 JJ Amsterdam,
The Netherlands
Tel/Fax: 0031-20-636-3915

## UNITED STATES

**The Reflexology Association of America**
4012 South Rainbow Boulevard, Box K585, Las Vegas,
Nevada 89103-2059, USA

## AUSTRALIA

**Reflexology Association of Australia**
PO Box 366, Cammeray, NSW 2062, Australia
Tel : (047) 214752

## INTERNET

www.britreflex.co.uk – the British Reflexology Association
www.reflexology-usa.org – the Reflexology Association of
America
www.ozemail.com.au/-raa – the Reflexology Association of
Australia
http://raa.inta.net.au – the Reflexology Association of
Australia
www.reflexology.org – the Home of Reflexology

COLLINS GEM
1950s
*a mine of information*

COLLINS GEM
1960s
*a mine of information*

COLLINS GEM
1970s
NO GAS
*a mine of information*

COLLINS GEM
1980s
*a mine of information*

COLLINS  Jane's
CIVIL
AIRCRAFT
*a mine of information*

COLLINS GEM
CLANS
& Tartans
*a mine of information*

COLLINS GEM
Classic
TV SERIES
*a mine of information*

COLLINS  Jane's
COMBAT
AIRCRAFT
*a mine of information*

COLLINS GEM
FIRSTS
*a mine of information*

COLLINS GEM
GOLF
*a mine of information*

COLLINS GEM
HILLWALKER'S
Survival Guide
*a mine of information*

COLLINS GEM
HOME
EMERGENCY GUIDE
*a mine of information*

COLLINS GEM
Collecting
STAMPS
*a mine of information*

COLLINS GEM
STARS
*a mine of information*

COLLINS GEM
SUPERSTITIONS
*a mine of information*

COLLINS GEM
Using Your
SOFTWARE
*a mine of information*